Activating Students' Ideas!

Acknowledgments

I would like to dedicate this book to Patricia Friedrichsen, Lloyd Borrow, and in memory of Sandra K. Abell. I will forever be grateful for the encouragement and support I received from my graduate advisors, which have helped me develop as a person and a scholar. My advisors' dedication to me and my fellow students has changed the landscape for science teaching and learning.

I appreciate the care and detail given to my writing by my present and past NSTA teams and especially to Claire Reinburg and Cathy Iammartino. I am to a great extent indebted to Emily Brady. Emily has a selfless leadership style aimed at bettering educational experiences for students through more informed and purposeful teaching.

And the following deserve thank-yous as well:

- To Jessica Fries-Gaither, Rodger Bybee, Jay McTighe, Janice Koch, Tim Blesse, and Robert Payo for being thought partners who are always willing to help develop ideas from a more practical pedagogical perspective.

- To the Fort Zumwalt School District for its continued support of my scholarly work. In particular, to Jen Waters, who is a forward-thinking leader in curriculum and instruction and in many ways applies *explore-before-explain* thinking to school administration and leadership; to Anne Green, whose knowledge of science education is only superseded by her unwavering passion to ensure all students have equal access to high-quality science/STEM learning; and to Marilyn Duvall, a compassionate leader and strong collaborator who works tirelessly to help elevate student learning and motivation to new heights.

- To my family, my reason—Cathy, Finn, and Lua.

—Pat Brown

To all the teachers who have given feedback on the probes and the response activities.

—Page Keeley

About the Authors

Dr. Patrick L. Brown is the executive director of STEAM and career education for the Fort Zumwalt School District in St. Charles, Missouri. Before arriving at Fort Zumwalt, he received a PhD in curriculum and instruction from the University of Missouri, Columbia. Dr. Brown has a range of K–12 and postsecondary teaching experience. He has taught elementary, middle level, and high school lessons, as well as both undergraduate and graduate courses for prospective elementary, middle, and high school teachers. He has won various awards for his science methods course teaching.

Known for his scholarship on instructional sequences to teach science, Dr. Brown makes frequent presentations at international, regional, and state conferences. He is the author of the bestselling NSTA book series *Instructional Sequence Matters*. His science teaching ideas have appeared in *Science and Children*, *Science Scope*, *The Science Teacher*, and *Science Activities*. His research in science education has been published in *Science Education*, the *Journal of Science Teacher Education*, and the *International Journal of Science Education*.

Page Keeley consults with school districts and organizations and is a frequently invited speaker at conferences throughout the United States and internationally, where she gives talks on building capacity for formative assessment and understanding student thinking. She has authored 22 books on formative assessment, curriculum topic study, and teaching for conceptual understanding. She is also a regular column contributor to the NSTA *Science and Children* journal, having authored over 60 articles on using formative assessment probes. Her *Uncovering Student Ideas in Science* series is used in hundreds of school districts and colleges across the United States and has received several distinguished awards.

Keeley holds a B.S. in life sciences from the University of New Hampshire and an M.Ed in science education from the University of Maine. After beginning her career as a research assistant in immunogenetics at the Jackson Laboratory in Bar Harbor, Maine, she became interested in teaching and learning and decided to pursue a career in education, teaching middle school and high school science in Maine for 14 years. She left the classroom in 1996 to focus on teacher professional learning. Keeley retired from the Maine Mathematics and Science Alliance, where she was the science program director for 16 years and a principal investigator and director of three NSF-funded projects. She also served as president of the National Science Teaching Association (NSTA) and the National Science Education Leadership Association (NSELA).

She has received several awards, including the Presidential Award for Secondary Science Teaching in 1992, the Milken National Educator Award in 1993, the Susan Loucks-Horsley Award for Leadership from Learning Forward in 2009, the Outstanding Leadership in Science Education Award from NSELA in 2013, and the Distinguished Service to Science Education Award from NSTA in 2017. She is a Cohort 1 fellow of the National Academy for Science Education Leadership.

Activating Students' Ideas

LINKING FORMATIVE ASSESSMENT PROBES
TO INSTRUCTIONAL SEQUENCE

Patrick Brown

Page Keeley

National Science Teaching Association

Cathy Iammartino, Director of Publications and Digital Initiatives

ART AND DESIGN
Will Thomas, Cover Design

PRINTING AND PRODUCTION
Colton Gigot, Senior Production Manager

DESIGN, PRODUCTION, AND PROJECT MANAGEMENT
KTD+ Education Group

NATIONAL SCIENCE TEACHING ASSOCIATION
Erika C. Shugart, PhD, Executive Director

405 E Laburnum Ave Ste 3, Richmond, VA 23222
NSTA.org/store
For customer service inquiries, please call 800-277-5300.

Cover image: graphixmania/Shutterstock. Lesson opener image: VerAtro/Shutterstock.

LIBRARY OF CONGRESS CATALOGING-IN-PUBLICATION DATA
Names: Brown, Patrick, 1978- author. | Keeley, Page, author.
Title: Activating students' ideas : linking formative assessment probes to instructional sequence / Patrick Brown, Page Keeley.
Description: Arlington, VA : National Science Teaching Association, [2023] | Includes bibliographical references and index.
Identifiers: LCCN 2022046395 (print) | LCCN 2022046396 (ebook) | ISBN 9781681409689 (paperback) | ISBN 9781681409696 (pdf)
Subjects: LCSH: Science--Study and teaching (Elementary) | Science--Study and teaching (Elementary)--Evaluation. | Teacher effectiveness. | Inquiry-based learning. | Next Generation Science Standards (Education)
Classification: LCC LB1585 .B688 2023 (print) | LCC LB1585 (ebook) | DDC 372.35/044--dc23/eng/20221102
LC record available at lccn.loc.gov/2022046395
LC ebook record available at lccn.loc.gov/2022046396

Contents

Foreword

Johannes Gutenberg's printing press was one of the most impactful inventions of all times. Before Gutenberg, all books had to be copied by hand or laboriously stamped out using woodblocks. Around 1450, Gutenberg coupled the flexibility of a coin punch with the power of a wine press to invent a printing device with movable type. His invention enabled the production of books and the spread of knowledge and ideas throughout the world. The printing press is but one example of the power of combinatorial thinking—linking two or more ideas or items to create something new and improved. Similarly, the authors of *Activating Students' Ideas* have fused key ideas from their respective careers to create a powerful integrative model for science teaching.

Both authors have distinguished themselves individually. Page Keeley has graced the field of science education through her seminal work on using formative assessment probes to activate students' prior knowledge and reveal any flawed preconceptions they may harbor. Patrick Brown's work on instructional sequencing operationalizes the often-cited aim of having students "doing" science as an evidence-based endeavor rather than simply learning science facts from didactic lectures and densely packed textbooks.

Together, Brown and Keeley weave together a pedagogical whole that exceeds its parts. Of course, their work has always been conceptually united around the science of learning that highlights the significant role of prior knowledge (including flawed preconceptions in science) in new learning and the benefits of actively engaging students in constructing new understandings. Not surprisingly, the ideas in *Activating Students' Ideas* align perfectly with the 3-D construct established by the *Next Generation Science Standards* (*NGSS*). In fact, the instructional approach the authors advocate unlocks the pedagogical door that has proven elusive for many science teachers struggling to implement the *NGSS*.

While the book is theoretically grounded in current research, the authors adroitly bridge from theory to practice. Indeed, the bulk of the book consists of a series of illustrative model lessons that concretize their ideas and offer a replicable instructional framework. As an added bonus, some of the lesson vignettes include videos of science learning in process, photographs of students' work, and reflective comments by learners.

In sum, the value of *Activating Students' Ideas* is based on a set of *if-then* propositions:

- IF you wish to apply the science of learning to your teaching of science…

- IF you understand the three-dimensional construct of the *NGSS* and wish to translate its aspirations to your classroom practice, and…

- IF you wish to enliven your teaching by engaging students in "doing" science…

THEN you have made a good decision to read this book and apply its ideas. Your teaching will be enriched, and your students will thank you for it.

—Jay McTighe
Coauthor of *Understanding by Design*
(ASCD, 2005)

Preface

For many elementary educators, teaching science is frequently a challenging task that can be intimidating. This book is an invitation to rethink the possibilities for learners and is intended to be a source of inspiration for new ways to think about science teaching. We have written this book to highlight the importance of sequencing science instruction to maximize learning and address the types of learning experiences called for in *A Framework for K–12 Science Education* (NRC 2012). While the *Framework* opens up many possible teaching approaches, we emphasize learning by doing science, which naturally combines the three dimensions of modern standards.

This book merges two widely used resources in elementary science: the *Uncovering Student Ideas in Science* series by Page Keeley and the *Instructional Sequence Matters* series by Patrick Brown. We have come together in this book to show how these resources work together to support student learning. The *Uncovering Student Ideas* series highlights the importance of using formative assessment probes to identify the variety of ideas students bring to the classroom and design instruction based on these preconceptions. Formative assessment plays a prominent role in science education, and emerging research in cognitive science emphasizes the importance of assessment-centered classrooms (Bransford, Brown, and Cocking 2000). Assessment-centered classrooms highlight the necessity of starting with students' ideas and teaching for transfer, as well as the critical role metacognition plays in developing deeper conceptual understanding. We believe that students' prior experiences and knowledge are critical assets. When we productively build on what students know and think and provide common classroom experiences with data that

serve as evidence for science sensemaking, students develop long-lasting and robust understanding. To provide students with common sensemaking experiences, we use the *Uncovering Student Ideas* formative assessment probes in an instructional sequence called *explore-before-explain*. *Explore-before-explain* acknowledges the pivotal role that active, experiential learning plays in the development of conceptual science understanding (Donovan and Bransford 2005). The explanations that students form are equally important, enabling them to develop a more sophisticated understanding and higher levels of science literacy.

While the term *explore-before-explain* may sound new, the approach is closely related to the BSCS 5E (Engage, Explore, Explain, Elaborate, Evaluate) Instructional Model (Bybee 1997). While others have written about the 5E (see Abell and Volkmann 2006), and the instructional sequence is a theme of many authors' National Science Teaching Association journal articles, our approach is consistent with their ideas but also unique. We have worked with many well-intentioned teachers whose background experiences and misconceptions about the phases and purposes hinder their ability to implement 5E instructional sequences (this is also supported by research; see Brown, Abell, and Friedrichsen 2013). Rather than cover all 5E phases, we chose *explore-before-explain* to scaffold teacher learning and focus on the constructivist types of instruction that *A Framework for K–12 Science Education* calls for.

You can build a stronger foundation for the *Uncovering Student Ideas in Science* series and *explore-before-explain* teaching by becoming familiar with the resources we provide to build your knowledge of effective teaching and learning. To learn more about these series, visit our websites at UncoveringStudentIdeas.org and PatBrownEdu.com

MAKING THE SHIFT TO *EXPLORE-BEFORE-EXPLAIN*

Many great resources and strategies are available to support student learning. Why did we choose to focus on the *explore-before-explain* instructional sequence? Many elementary science teachers we work with already value and use a hands-on approach to student learning; however, the placement of their explorations and explanations may not leverage the best learning possible. Hands-on or experiential learning approaches in which students engage in activities after a concept, idea, or phenomenon has been explained may not be optimal from a learning standpoint. However, this can be a good starting point for becoming an *explore-before-explain* teacher. Rather than asking you to toss out everything you have been doing and build something new from scratch, we focus on helping you think about instructional sequence, Making the simple shift in your teaching approach to reverse the order of students' hands-on experiences can have a significant impact on learners. Becoming an *explore-before-explain* teacher requires innovation and modification of your existing instructional design. Whether you use an iterative approach (altering something that currently exists) or an inventive approach (creating something new), the goal is to create a better instructional sequence for students by starting with exploratory experiences and explaining. Throughout this book, we attempt to cultivate and grow your knowledge, skills, and strategies to help you shift your current instructional sequences into *explore-before-explain* student experiences.

We have worked with many science educators, ranging from classroom teachers to science specialists who support teachers, and are often confronted with questions like "What would it take to accomplish learning growth for every student, every year?" and "What does it look like when students have developed deep conceptual understanding?" Several key factors must be in place to commit to a new mindset and instructional approach:

1. We must view our learning as dynamic and evolving (growth mindset) versus fixed and unchangeable (fixed mindset).

2. We have to understand our own beliefs about teaching and learning to make sense of new pedagogical practices.

3. We must honestly believe that all students can learn and construct conceptual understanding at high levels.

4. We must have a manageable plan to implement our vision of good teaching and learning. Overly challenging or multiple unrelated plans can be difficult to implement.

5. We must align curriculum, instruction, assessment practices, and ties to other areas (e.g., mathematics, English language arts, social studies) with consistency.

6. We need to rethink current structures instead of adding on to what already exists.

WHO WILL THIS BOOK HELP AND HOW?

Regardless of their level of experience, from novice to expert, educators can read, discuss, implement, and dissect each model lesson to better understand how the sequence of science instruction promotes deeper and long-lasting understanding. Beginning teachers can use the model lessons to build a repertoire of research-based strategies to improve student learning during their first years of teaching. Experienced teachers who already value hands-on approaches but find that their lessons fall slightly short in influencing students the way they intended can benefit from the simple reorganization of instruction. Teacher educators and professional developers can easily implement these lessons to model best practices in science education.

This book provides a self-guided professional learning experience. Through reading and discussing the chapters, teachers can gain valuable insight into why some approaches may be more beneficial than others. While professional development highlights the need for educators to grow individually, professional learning retools this idea so that teachers are learning how to serve students better. Teachers have real-life examples and a rationale for restructuring the hands-on approaches they are currently using. To make the shift and become experts at the approach described in this book, teachers will need time to think about the sequence of science instruction and its connection to the *Framework*. It's also important to keep in mind that implementing the *explore-before-explain* sequence may not go perfectly right from the start. Our goal is for teachers to read the chapters, reflect on their practices, learn from the examples, and start creating lessons that meet the vision described in *A Framework for K–12 Science Education*.

REFERENCES

Abell, S. K., and M. J. Volkmann. 2006. *Seamless assessments in science: A guide for elementary and middle school teachers.* Arlington, VA: NSTA Press.

Bransford, J., A. Brown, and R. Cocking. 2000. *How people learn: Brain, mind, experience, and school.* Washington, DC: National Academies Press.

Brown, P., P. Friedrichsen, and S. Abell. 2013. The development of prospective secondary biology teachers' PCK. *Journal of Science Teacher Education* 24 (1): 133–155.

Bybee, R. W. 1997. *Achieving scientific literacy: From purposes to practices.* Portsmouth, NH: Heinemann Educational Books.

Donovan, M. S., and J. D. Bransford, eds. 2005. *How students learn: Science in the classroom.* Washington, DC: National Academies Press.

National Research Council (NRC). 2012. *A framework for K–12 science education: Practices, crosscutting concepts, and core ideas.* Washington, DC: National Academies Press.

Introduction

When we want to build a sturdy house, we choose durable materials that we hope will last a lifetime. Once the foundation has been poured, people often don't give it another thought. Without solid groundwork, however, the walls will crumble and there will be nothing to support a roof. Similarly, you cannot expect students to develop deeper conceptual understanding without a foundation supported by firsthand experiences with data as evidence for sensemaking. Just as in any construction project, you might need to slow down, refurbish specific components, and renovate to modernize. Teaching for conceptual understanding may take some time, but it is well worth the payoff.

Our approach to curriculum design is analogous to building a house. We propose a fundamental *if-then* proposition to curriculum planning and implementation. *If* the primary goal of modern science education is to equip students to transfer their learning to new situations, *then* teachers should design a curriculum to promote conceptual understanding with chances for authentic performances of transfer, rather than create long lists of discrete topics or skills to cover. Planning for conceptual understanding focuses on teaching the most crucial science concepts and practices, logical thinking skills, and the best use of instructional time (McTighe and Silver 2020). The desired conceptual understanding from firsthand experience is the foundation on which student knowledge is built. By using curriculum focused around big ideas, teachers can go into greater depth and students can develop a more sophisticated understanding.

A Framework for K–12 Science Education: Practices, Crosscutting Concepts, and Core Ideas (NRC 2012) emphasizes teaching for a deeper understanding of concepts versus superficially covering vast amounts of information. Konicek-Moran and Keeley (2015) describe what it means for students to build conceptual understanding:

> When students have an understanding of a concept, they can (a) think with it, (b) use it in areas other than that in which they learned it, (c) state it in their own words, (d) find a metaphor or an analogy for it, or (e) build a mental or physical model of it. In other words, the students have made the concept their own. (p. 6)

BIG IDEA #1

Students who have conceptual understanding can use ideas to understand their world in many ways.

Focusing on fewer, more significant ideas is critical to avoid superficial coverage while allowing more time to engage students in the kinds of active, meaning-making processes necessary for developing conceptual understandings. Said a bit differently, knowledge acquisition alone is insufficient; schools need to develop students' know-how and knowing abilities. Focusing on student understanding and transfer does not mean that educators should ignore basic skills or refrain from teaching factual knowledge. Basic knowledge and skills are fundamental, and students cannot apply what they have learned if they lack the basics. However, the basics should be considered the floor, not the ceiling, in modern education.

THE RESEARCH SUPPORT FOR TEACHING FOR CONCEPTUAL UNDERSTANDING AND TRANSFER LEARNING

Teaching for conceptual understanding and transfer resides on a single premise with far-reaching implications: If we want to produce more powerful learning for students, then we need to ground our practice in current research on teaching and learning. Using the *Uncovering Student Ideas* formative assessment probes and designing instruction should relate to what we know about the best possible learning environments. *How People Learn* (Bransford, Brown, and Cocking 2000) and *How People Learn II: Learners, Contexts, and Cultures* (NASEM 2018) describe three interrelated factors that are essential for ensuring high-quality classroom instruction: learner, knowledge, and assessment.

Learner-Centered Instruction

Fundamental to learner-centered instruction is the idea that all knowledge is constructed through active experience. This means that knowledge is not passively received. The learner-centered principle is rooted in a long-held constructivist epistemology that acknowledges that students learn science best when they actively construct knowledge that builds on prior understanding based on firsthand experiences with data and evidence. This may seem like a simple idea, but it is not. The best active, learner-centered lessons provide experiences that deeply entrench ideas and promote long-lasting understanding. In this regard, the understanding is highlighted by an individual's ability to reconstruct and apply conceptual knowledge rather than to retrieve specific facts (NASEM 2018). Long-lasting understanding is promoted when learners construct knowledge, connect details within a broader framework for understanding, and relate information to the knowledge they already have.

Learner-centered environments are mediated by teachers and student-to-student experiences that make thinking and learning explicit for students. Learner-centered instruction describes a complex interaction among students' prior knowledge and experiences, new individual and group experiences, and reflecting and thinking about their developing understanding, termed *metacognition*. Students come to school as knowers even before being taught anything. They have lived for some years and constructed ideas about how the world works from their everyday interactions with their environment, family, and friends, as well as from media. They have become knowers through their firsthand experiences that provide evidence for their ideas. The ideas they have constructed serve as the framework from which they try to advance their understanding. How students think about their ideas, and how they monitor and reflect on their developing understanding, is critical for regulating and being more self-reliant (NASEM 2018).

If students' knowledge is rooted in alternative conceptions, it can become a barrier to future learning. Examples of alternative preconceived ideas students may hold about science are well documented in the K–5 science education and research literature. These include broad thoughts and many specific, more nuanced ideas involving life and living processes (e.g., living things, nutrition, genetics, inheritance), materials and their properties (e.g., solids, liquids, and gases; chemical changes; particles), and physical processes (e.g., electricity, magnetism, energy) (see Driver et al. 1994). Because students' incoming ideas serve as the foundation for future learning, they are a critical consideration in planning. Engaging in evidence-based experiences and reflecting on developing understanding can help students overcome alternative preconceptions, generally referred to as *misconceptions*. Learner-centered environments help students construct accurate understanding from data-producing experiences, along with interactions with teachers and peers.

Finally, the learner-centeredness of an environment is influenced by the individual's upbringing. How learners grow and learn is related to their cultural, social cognitive, and biological contexts (NASEM 2018). Learning is influenced fundamentally by students' home environments, and the difficulties they encounter may be due to a mismatch between their cultural experiences and the expectations at school. The cultural influence on learning goes beyond *what* students learn to include *how* they learn (Brown and Abell 2007a). Thus, classrooms should be learner-centered environments that highlight activating students' prior knowledge and engaging them in active experiences that promote developing understanding.

Knowledge-Centered Instruction

If, as learners, students all try to integrate new experiences with prior knowledge, it follows that they learn most readily if the targeted ideas fit within a broader framework for what they should know and be able to do at a specific grade level or band. Knowledge-centered classrooms focus on the types of ideas, practices, and skills students will encounter and how these ideas should be organized to optimize learning. The process of creating knowledge-centered classrooms requires us to evaluate our teaching environment. Essential questions come to mind when assessing the knowledge-centeredness of our science classrooms: Is the subject matter aligned with the appropriate standards? Is the topic connected to more prominent, overarching ideas? Is skill development focused on advancing abilities and how to use them over time?

Students' knowledge at different ages and grade levels is well researched. Four significant documents guiding science education have been released over

the past few decades in the United States: *Benchmarks for Science Literacy* (AAAS 1993), *National Science Education Standards* (NRC 1996), *A Framework for K–12 Science Education* (NRC 2012), and *Next Generation Science Standards* (*NGSS* Lead States 2013). These guiding documents used current science teaching and learning research to set goals for the types of knowledge, skills, and abilities students should gain from classroom instruction. A knowledge-centered environment introduces knowledge components (e.g., concepts, facts, skills, science practices, reflection on thinking) promptly when the need for knowledge emerges or students need them. A knowledge-centered environment guides students in learning for long-lasting understanding and helps them transfer their abilities to new and different areas.

Assessment-Centered Instruction

Finally, teaching for optimal understanding requires an assessment-centered classroom. Such classrooms focus on high standards for learning and provide frequent feedback so that students can self-monitor their developing understanding at all stages of development. Feedback comes in many forms and includes assessing students' development of ideas within a discipline of study (e.g., science content and practices used to generate knowledge) and aiding them in becoming more independent learners. Also, feedback comes at different points in time during the learning process.

The importance of feedback is the subject of many resources for teachers. For instance, in *Understanding by Design*, Wiggins and McTighe (2005) argue that learning goals and assessments should be developed before designing instructional activities. Their backward design framework attempts to help teachers zero in on essential knowledge in a unit of study and then design activities to aid students in learning new ideas and developing their abilities.

Formative feedback is ongoing and used to help students monitor their developing understanding and take measures of what they have learned and what areas they still find confusing. Summative feedback enables teachers to determine whether individuals and classes as a whole have gained needed knowledge at the end of a unit of study and makes students aware of where they stand. Finally, assessment-centered classrooms help students isolate the knowledge and skills they need to develop to reach their peak academic abilities.

The Classroom Learning Culture

The principles underlying *How People Learn* and *How People Learn II* do not operate in isolation but are overlapping and deeply entrenched to form the classroom's learning culture (see Figure 1). While we have described them as separate entities, the best learning environments operate at the nexus of the principles of learner-, assessment-, and knowledge-centered classrooms. For example, the feedback advocated by assessment-centered classrooms directly influences learners and their ability to reflect on their developing understanding. The knowledge and standards used to design instruction have a direct impact on the activities chosen to help students construct knowledge. Finally, the standards selected to guide instruction should closely align with the evaluations used to assess student understanding. The ideas underlying *How People Learn* and *How People Learn II* show that a holistic approach is necessary to accommodate the intricacies of learning.

Figure 1. *Components and Their Attributes of How Students Learn Best*

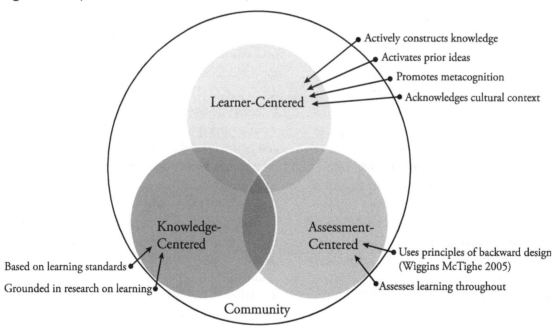

Sources: Bransford, Brown, and Cocking 2000; NASEM 2018

BUILDING A FOUNDATION OF CONCEPTUAL UNDERSTANDING THROUGH *EXPLORE-BEFORE-EXPLAIN* INSTRUCTIONAL SEQUENCES

Advances in cognitive learning theory lend valuable insights into what students can do and how teachers should plan instruction according to how students best learn science. *Explore-before-explain* teaching aligns with cognitive science research and emphasizes that a student's construction of knowledge creates a framework for developing understanding. The hallmark of *explore-before-explain* is sequencing instruction so students build their experiences and knowledge through using data and evidence before developing explanations. Said a bit differently, *explore-before-explain* lessons ensure that a student's conceptual understanding is primarily built on evidence-based experiences.

Historically, teachers have often played the role of content deliverers to students, who are considered receptacles to be filled with knowledge. The passive role of students is underscored in the instructional script used in teacher-directed classrooms where teacher explanation of content comes first, followed by verification and practice-type activities (Hofstein and Lunetta 2004). This approach fails to promote the logical and critical thinking about data needed to articulate the evidence used to explain a concept or phenomenon. Furthermore, this teaching sequence of telling followed by verification activities where the outcome is already known to students does little to help them disentangle misconceptions or fill in the gaps of partially developed ideas. These misconceptions may be grounded in what seems reasonable to the students but are unsubstantiated by empirical evidence and do not accurately depict science (Duschl, Schweingruber, and Shouse 2007). Finally, this passive sequence of instruction places students at the receiving end of learning as recipients of knowledge, confirm-

ing and practicing ideas, as opposed to an active sequence of instruction in which students are doing the intellectual work of constructing knowledge from firsthand experiences. Arguably, being on the receiving end of learning in a classroom does not prepare students to succeed in a knowledge-driven, science-literate society that requires critical thinking and problem-solving.

If our goal is to prepare students to be participants in a world shaped by science and technology, then the passive classroom experience must change to a classroom with active experiences in which students are engaged in sensemaking and knowledge construction, discarding ideas that are no longer supported by evidence. Focusing on "inert" knowledge, which students seldom understand deeply, is replaced by active learning, where students' firsthand experiences, using scientific practices, serve as their conceptual framework for understanding the fundamental ideas of science. Lessons need to be artfully crafted to allow for "just-in-time learning" and the gradual unfolding and elaborating of ideas through experiences that build a conceptual bridge between students' initial ideas and the scientific understandings that help them make sense of their world. More specifically, teachers facilitate and guide knowledge development, rather than dispense it, by purposefully using a well-designed instructional sequence, such as *explore-before-explain*, to construct and elaborate on ideas over time. Indeed, research supports these assertions, and scholarship in science education shows that *explore-before-explain* instructional sequences lead to deeper, long-lasting understanding (Bybee et al. 2006; Brown and Abell 2007b).

BIG IDEA #2

The *explore-before-explain* sequence is an active process that promotes consistency in learning through the gradual unfolding of ideas.

Leveraging the Assets All Students Bring to Class

How we set up early learning around an idea is critical. All students come to school as knowers even before being taught anything. Each student arrives with unique assets, including their everyday experiences interacting with the natural world, curiosities, interests, cultures, and abilities. We can leverage these assets to better understand the ideas students bring to the classroom and use them to create everyday learning experiences that use data as evidence for sensemaking. One of these assets, the preconceptions students bring to their learning, influences how they make sense of the concepts and phenomena they encounter in the science classroom. Preconceptions can consist of accurate knowledge and partially developed ideas or scientifically flawed misconceptions.

Using the *Uncovering Student Ideas* formative assessment probes helps teachers elicit student understandings, but these probes also do so much more. Each formative assessment probe identifies a relevant phenomenon with which to start a new lesson and creates a "need-to-know" situation for students. The research on emotions and attention suggests that these develop in parallel streams. When new learning has an emotional component, the chance increases that it will be stored in long-term memory (Sousa and Tomlinson 2011). Students' predictions or hypotheses about the assessment probes engage the brain from a cognitive angle, initiating a flood of neurobiological processes. Neurologist and teacher Judy Willis contends that prediction is one of the highest-yield instructional strategies, since it focuses the brain's attention and sets up a need to know (McTighe and Willis 2019). If a prediction is successful, this validates prior knowledge and sound reasoning. If the prediction is incorrect, the brain wants to discover why and seeks an explanation. Incorrect ideas and predictions are essential from a cognitive standpoint, because only if students find new ideas more compelling do they change and begin to revise their initial conceptions and create new theories about how the world works.

Learning may not always be easy, but the challenge is a positive sign of stretching understanding. Studies on students' misconceptions support this claim and have shown that teaching is likely ineffective unless it considers learners' perspectives (Driver et al. 1994). Thus, preassessment time should be used not just to elicit prior content knowledge and experiences but also to familiarize students with their strengths, past experiences, and interests related to the topic under study.

BIG IDEA #3

Starting with students' incoming ideas lays the foundation for learning and sets up a need-to-know classroom learning environment.

Using Data as Evidence for Sensemaking

When students have to think about and reconcile the difference between their preconceptions and the data they collect and analyze through carefully designed instruction, they build a conceptual bridge between their initial ideas and the scientific ideas that help them make sense of their natural world. Thus, regardless of the accuracy of their incoming ideas, all students are on a sequential path to developing conceptual understanding grounded in learning science by doing.

The exploration phase allows students to draw on their current understanding to investigate questions or solve problems. Studies on the cognition of early learning show that kids' play is often an attempt to understand things, similarly to the way scientists learn through experimentation (Gopnik, Meltzoff, and Kuhl 1999). In the *explore-before-explain* classroom, students investigate natural phenomena, have questions about how things work, and collect information. They use intelligence-gathering practices to learn about science and test their prior experiences. All the while, students rely on pattern recognition and cause-and-effect relationships to develop a deeper understanding. This is an iterative process, and students learn about the likelihood of something happening based on another event occurring. As a result, learning is rapid when new understanding is dependent on prior data-producing experiences, and students can draw rich inferences from sparse data in a short amount of time.

Make all learning about the process. Students need the opportunity to collect data, analyze these data, and determine how to make sense of what the data may mean. Students can elevate their developing understanding by thinking about the validity and reliability of their experience and the information collected. Students should consider what differences in the data, if any, they might find if they completed the investigation again. They should consider the convergence and divergence of data points. Finally, they should scrutinize outlying data points, for these may be the result of a fundamental difference that merits further exploration or of a misstep in the procedure, measuring device, or measurement.

Only when students analyze data and then interpret what the analysis means about the science they are exploring do they have evidence. The practice

of having students generate knowledge transforms their experience from a passive to an active meaning-making experience. In this way, we level the playing field for all students. Decades of studies have shown that students develop a deeper understanding and retain that understanding longer when they actively construct explanations (McNeill and Krajcik 2012).

BIG IDEA #4

Students who translate *data → evidence → scientific claim* perform difficult intellectual work like scientists. When students find patterns and causal relationships in the data, they have evidence for science sensemaking.

Facilitating Understanding Through Productive Discourse

Students are not alone in the process and are part of a larger scientific culture—their classroom—which grows based on the collective work of all the students. To extend the house analogy, our work as architects helps connect our blueprints for the lessons we design with on-the-spot sensemaking during the build process. During students' formation of ideas, the teacher is a guide who asks probing and clarifying questions to get students to use data as evidence to better explain their thinking (Lemke 1990). The role of the teacher is to help students make sense of the scientific phenomenon. In some ways, the teacher may seem like an interviewer. As interviewers, we listen closely to students' ideas and help them formulate clear lines of arguments about the science under study. The goal is to help students select ideas, make critical connections between ideas, and shape ideas. Teachers that promote productive scientific discourse in the classroom are purposeful. Throughout the process, they check student understanding by asking probing questions and seeking clarification statements (e.g., "Why did you select *this* idea?" "How does the data serve as evidence for *this* idea?" "How does the evidence support the claim you are making?"). Quickly moving on to something new without providing talk time may slow down students' development of conceptual understanding. Even worse, their ideas may fade from their minds.

This seems like a simple idea, but it is not, as it involves many different considerations. First, to develop and refine ideas in our planning, we must provide students time to think, talk, and write. Long-lasting understanding is built when learners construct knowledge, connect details within a broader framework for understanding, and relate information with the experience they already have. The depth of students' conceptual understanding will be related to how tightly supporting ideas are connected to their framework for understanding. From a neurobiological standpoint, having students talk about the patterns in the data they are using as evidence helps create meaningful connections between neurons via synapses. Synapses are not fixed bridges between neurons and can change over time based on experiences and new inputs. Synapses that are being used are strengthened, while those not being used or are not particularly helpful are pruned away. The process is analogous to pruning a rosebush, in which the weaker branches are removed (pruned away) so the more significant branches can grow stronger. Synaptic pruning is a way to streamline neural circuits to boost knowledge and skills for adulthood. (Blakemore 2010; Blakemore and Choudhury 2006).

BIG IDEA #5

How students talk with each other and with teachers is pivotal for developing and refining understanding.

Addressing Contemporary Standards

A Framework for K–12 Science Education (NRC 2012) and the *Next Generation Science Standards* (*NGSS*) (*NGSS* Lead States 2013), which are based on the *Framework*, aim to shift instruction so that students can take a more active role in learning. Throughout this book, we show how using the *Uncovering Student Ideas* formative assessment probes in an *explore-before-explain* sequence supports the vision of teaching and learning described in contemporary science standards. The *Framework* advocates intertwining disciplinary core ideas (DCIs), science and engineering practices (SEPs), and crosscutting concepts (CCCs) to form opportunities for what is called three-dimensional teaching and learning. While each of these dimensions is critical on its own, they work together to support students' developing understanding.

The three dimensions have been analogized to threads that are woven or braided together into a rope, creating a larger and stronger form (*NGSS* Lead States 2013). The dimensions can be combined in different ways in curriculum and instruction and do not stand alone. In other words, when students are learning content, DCIs are combined with an SEP. SEPs are not taught alone as separate process skills; they are always combined with a DCI. Moreover, a third dimension, the CCCs, help unify students' understanding across disciplinary boundaries. Several states have created their new standards based on the *Framework* and have developed three-dimensional standards similar to the *NGSS* performance expectations for assessment. Becoming familiar with the three dimensions of the *Framework* can help you determine the shifts you need to make to use the *Uncovering Student Ideas* formative assessment probes in an *explore-before-explain* instructional sequence. Each dimension is briefly described below and summarized in Table 1.

Science and Engineering Practices: The SEPs require students to mesh skills that scientists and engineers use, such as questioning, developing and using models, investigation, explanation construction, and problem-solving, to develop new content ideas (Bybee 2012). The *Framework* identifies eight SEPs that are essential in a K–12 science and engineering curriculum and are taught in the context of the content students are learning (NRC 2012) (see Table 1). These eight practices embody the

Table 1. *A Summary of the Three Dimensions of the NGSS*

Science and Engineering Practices	Crosscutting Concepts
1. Asking questions and defining problems	1. Patterns
2. Developing and using models	2. Cause and effect
3. Planning and carrying out investigations	3. Scale, proportion, and quantity
4. Analyzing and interpreting data	4. Systems and system models
5. Using mathematics and computational thinking	5. Energy and matter
6. Constructing explanations and designing solutions	6. Structure and function
7. Engaging in argument from evidence	7. Stability and change
8. Obtaining, evaluating	

Disciplinary Core Ideas			
Physical Science	**Life Sciences**	**Earth and Space Sciences**	**Engineering, Technology, and the Application of Science**
PS 1: Matter and its interactions	LS 1: From molecules to organisms: Structures and processes	ESS 1: Earth's place in the universe	ETS 1: Engineering design
PS 2: Motion and stability: Forces and interactions	LS 2: Ecosystems: Interactions, energy, and dynamics	ESS 2: Earth's systems	ETS 2: Links among engineering, technology, science, and society
PS 3: Energy	LS 3: Heredity: Inheritance and variation of traits	ESS 3: Earth and human activity	
PS 4: Waves and their applications in technologies for information transfer	LS 4: Biological evaluation: Unity and diversity		

multifaceted, overlapping processes that scientists use to develop and share knowledge about the natural world. As students use these practices in the *explore-before-explain* sequence of instruction, they generate knowledge and come to understand how knowledge is generated in science.

Crosscutting Concepts: The CCCs provide an organizational framework for helping students connect knowledge from different disciplines of science. They aid students in gaining a deeper understanding because of their explanatory power, connecting knowledge from disciplines to a coherent and scientifically based view of the world (NRC 2012). The *Framework* identifies seven CCCs spanning disciplinary boundaries (Duschl 2012) (see Table 1). These CCCs help students focus their thinking on particular aspects of a phenomenon.

Disciplinary Core Ideas: The DCIs include statements of scientific ideas used to understand and explain natural and human-designed phenomena around four core areas: physical sciences, life science, Earth and space sciences, and engineering technology and the application of science. Within each core area are DCIs, which describe the content central to each discipline and necessary for students to develop proficiency (see Table 1).

BIG IDEA #6

The three dimensions of the *Framework* emerge naturally when the *Uncovering Student Ideas* formative assessment probes are used in an *explore-before-explain* instructional sequence.

Conclusions

Teaching for greater conceptual understanding is complex. Although at this point, your mind may be spinning with questions and ideas, the main thing to remember is to make all learning about the process. The more you can layer what you know about the best educational environments, the more effective you will be at boosting students' capacity to become more self-reliant learners. Research supports this claim, and developing expertise in employing *explore-before-explain* instructional sequences means recognizing patterns that allow for easy retrieval and translation of ideas (Bransford, Brown, and Cocking 2000). This is a time to show students where they are heading in the process. Students need to be encouraged to view their prior understandings as building blocks to academic success instead of setbacks. We can do this by not viewing incoming student ideas as something negative, but rather taking the perspective that variations in classroom ideas prime growth and development. Regardless of the accuracy of incoming ideas, students can help each other grow and become more scientifically minded. Students need to learn the intrinsic rewards and satisfaction of growing through the learning process, which starts with understanding their ideas and how they are formed. From a learning and neurobiological standpoint, the process is reciprocal: Brain development influences learning, and learning influences brain development (NASEM 2018).

REFERENCES

American Association for the Advancement of Science (AAAS). 1993. *Benchmarks for science literacy.* New York: Oxford University Press.

Blakemore, S.-J. 2010. The developing social brain: Implications for education. *Neuron* 65 (6): 744–747.

Blakemore, S.-J., and S. Choudhury. 2006. Development of the adolescent brain: Implications for executive function and social cognition. *Journal of Child Psychology and Psychiatry* 47 (3–4): 296–312.

Bransford, J., A. Brown, and R. Cocking. 2000. *How people learn: Brain, mind, experience, and school.* Washington, DC: National Academies Press.

Brown, P., and S. Abell. 2007a. Cultural diversity in the science classroom. *Science and Children* 44 (9): 60–61.

Brown, P., and S. Abell. 2007b. Examining the learning cycle. *Science and Children* 44 (5): 58–59.

Bybee, R. 2012. Scientific and engineering practices in K–12 classrooms: *Understanding A Framework for K–12 Science Education. The Science Teacher* 78 (9): 34–40.

Bybee, R. W., J. A. Taylor, A. Gardner, P. Van Scotter, J. C. Powell, A. Westbrook, and N. Landes. 2006. T*he BSCS 5E instructional model: Origins, effectiveness, and applications.* Colorado Springs, CO: BSCS. https://media.bscs.org/bscsmw/5es/bscs_5e_full_report.pdf.

Driver, R., A. Squires, P. Rushworth, and V. Wood-Robinson. 1994. *Making sense of secondary science: Research into children's ideas.* London: Routledge.

Duschl, R. A. 2012. The second dimension: Crosscutting concepts. *The Science Teacher* 79 (2): 34–38.

Duschl, R. A., H. A. Schweingruber, and A. W. Shouse, eds. 2007. *Taking science to school: Learning and teaching science in grades K–8.* Washington, DC: National Academies Press.

Gopnik, A., A. Meltzoff, and P. K. Kuhl. 1999. *The scientist in the crib: Minds, brains, and how children learn.* New York: William Morrow.

Hofstein, A., and V. N. Lunetta. 2004. The laboratory in science education: Foundation for the 21st century. *Science Education* 88 (1): 28–54.

Konicek-Moran, R., and P. Keeley 2015. *Teaching for conceptual understanding in science.* Arlington, VA: NSTA Press.

Lemke, J. L. 1990. *Talking science: Language, learning, and values.* Norwood, NJ: Ablex.

McNeill, K. L., and J. S. Krajcik. 2012. Supporting grade 5-8 students in constructing explanations in science: The claim, evidence, and reasoning framework for talk and writing. Upper Saddle River, NJ: Pearson.

McTighe, J., and H. Silver. 2020. Teaching for deeper learning: Tools to engage students in meaning making. Alexandria, VA: ASCD.

McTighe, J., and J. Willis 2019. Upgrade your teaching: Understanding by design meets neuroscience. Alexandria, VA: ASCD.

National Academies of Sciences, Engineering, and Medicine (NASEM). 2018. *How people learn II: Learners, contexts, and cultures.* Washington, DC: National Academies Press.

National Research Council (NRC). 1996. *National science education standards*. Washington, DC: National Academies Press.

National Research Council (NRC). 2012. *A framework for K–12 science education: Practices, crosscutting concepts, and core ideas*. Washington, DC: National Academies Press.

NGSS Lead States. 2013. *Next Generation Science Standards: For states, by states*. Washington, DC: National Academies Press. NextGenScience.org/next-generation-science-standards.

Sousa, D. A., and C. A. Tomlinson. 2011. *Differentiation and the brain: How neuroscience supports the learner-friendly classroom*. Bloomington, IN: Solution Tree Press.

Wiggins, G., and J. McTighe. 2005. *Understanding by design*. Expanded 2nd ed. Alexandria, VA: ASCD.

Exploring the Model Lessons

The model lessons have been designed with and taught to elementary students to illustrate how the *Uncovering Student Ideas* formative assessment probes and *explore-before-explain* teaching are a natural fit for addressing modern learning theory and the big ideas described in the introductory chapter. We have chosen a variety of physical, life, and Earth and space science model lessons to illustrate that the approach cuts across disciplines. The format provided in each model lesson will help you design lessons that incorporate the three dimensions described in *A Framework for K–12 Science Education* (NRC 2012). Each model lesson includes a brief introduction, materials list, *Uncovering Student Ideas* formative assessment probe with a teacher explanation, connections to the three dimensions of the *Framework*, a classroom vignette, and more. In this section, we offer some additional guidance on using the model lessons to reflect on current practices and develop *explore-before-explain* lessons that include the *Uncovering Student Ideas* formative assessment probes.

SUGGESTIONS FOR EMBEDDING PROBES IN INSTRUCTION

In the model lessons, the formative assessment probes are meant to engage student thinking and translate into firsthand experiences with data that serve as evidence for science sensemaking. Remember, one of the big ideas discussed in the introductory chapter is that "starting with students' incoming ideas lays the foundation for learning and sets up a need-to-know classroom learning environment." Thus, students bring valuable assets to the classroom, and you can use these assets to develop deeper conceptual understanding. From a learning and cognition standpoint, it is well worth the effort to elicit students' initial ideas and use them as springboards to learning at the onset of instruction. The probes create a need-to-know situation for students, motivating them to test their ideas. The probes should initiate *explore-before-explain* lessons and make students' thinking explicit before instruction. Students' initial ideas will also be essential benchmarks for their reflection on developing understanding and learning by doing science. Revisit the probes often during instruction to revise their ideas based on their experiences.

Another big idea from the introductory chapter is that "students who have conceptual understanding can use ideas to understand their world in many ways." It is important to use productive science discourse to help develop students' conceptual understanding. Make the probes about a classroom culture of ideas rather than correct answers. Continually stress, "What is our best thinking?" Make students aware that their ideas may change as they gather more evidence. Ask students to reflect on their experiences in order to describe where they got their ideas. You want them to consider how data-based experiences serve as evidence for understanding. As students work to pinpoint why their ideas changed, the ideas become refined and are more scientifically based due to their experiences. The importance of talk time cannot be overstated. As students talk through their developing understanding, they are developing a rich framework of conceptual understanding, and any small gaps in their knowledge may be discussed using data as evidence.

USING THE TEACHER EXPLANATIONS

The teacher explanations accompanying the probes provide a brief background of the content addressed, including the best answers and scientific explanations. We realize that many elementary teachers have not had significant science coursework, and their prior experiences may be considerably different from the *explore-before-explain* approach. We do not want our approach to be intimidating, so we have included the necessary information for each model lesson to support teachers' content knowledge. This section is meant to provide you with the knowledge base from which to ask probing questions and help students clarify their understanding from firsthand experiences. For each model lesson, the teacher explanation section elaborates on the science in the DCIs related to the lesson. In addition, research support is provided so you will be aware of common misconceptions for students at various grade spans. While the research should be helpful for all teachers, novice to experienced, if you have never taught this content before, this section provides examples of typical ways students think about the content and might answer the probes. The explanations can help you decide when the content is best taught and think about how you can link the scientific ideas in the probe to other ideas in your course.

USING THE *FRAMEWORK* CONNECTIONS

The connections to the *Framework* are made in two ways. First, a summary is presented of the disciplinary core ideas, science and engineering practices, and crosscutting concepts from the *Framework* that are relevant to the lesson. Second, each lesson includes a section connecting the *Framework*, *Uncovering Student Ideas* formative assessment probe, and the essential phases of the *explore-before-explain* instructional

sequence. The interplay between DCIs, teaching and learning, and formative assessment is key to using the lessons in this book and developing unique *explore-before-explain* lessons using the *Uncovering Student Ideas* formative assessment probes. The connections sections each illustrate a big idea from the introductory chapter, and the three dimensions of the *Framework* naturally emerge when using the *Uncovering Student Ideas* formative assessment probes in the *explore-before-explain* sequence. It is not uncommon for teachers to notice additional connections to the three dimensions of the *Framework* or have ideas for how to include other essential elements in the lesson. The dimensions of the *Framework* are situated in the experiences teachers choose for students and the instructional approaches they use during the *explore-before-explain* sequence. The connections we have made are clear to us; however, you should feel free to modify the connections in your practices to best meet your local curriculum and standards as long as you retain the *explore-before-explain* sequence of instruction.

USING THE MODEL LESSON VIGNETTES

The model lesson vignettes each provide a detailed description of how the lesson played out with students. The vignettes detail the types of teacher and student activities that occur during the essential phases of the *explore-before-explain* instructional sequence. We designed the vignettes to tie together all the big ideas from the introductory chapter and illustrate how using the *Uncovering Student Ideas* formative assessment probes in an *explore-before-explain* sequence aligns with contemporary cognitive science research. Some teachers may find it helpful to code the vignettes for their learner-, knowledge-, and assessment-centeredness. In professional learning experiences, we frequently take educators through the model lessons the way students experience them in the classroom. While doing so, we often stop to illustrate how the model lesson connects to the research-based big ideas in the lesson. This explicit connection helps teachers reflect on practices they are already doing or may need to emphasize to take student learning to new levels.

We realize that the process of becoming an *explore-before-explain* teacher using the *Uncovering Student Ideas* formative assessment probes may take some time. Research from *The Cambridge Handbook of Expertise and Expert Performance* recognizes that developing knowledge is most meaningful if integrated into practice (Ericsson et al. 2006). Therefore, to become experts, teachers need time to think about the sequence of science instruction and the *Framework*, and they probably will not implement the model lessons perfectly right from the start.

We have included a design template to reinforce the research and design considerations needed to provide *explore-before-explain* experiences and help you reflect on the essential elements as you read the model lessons (see Table 2). The template can also help you easily align your lessons with the three dimensions of the *Framework*.

Finally, when available, the vignettes include pictures of student work, student quotes, and video examples of how to perform some investigations and demonstrations. Student work and quotes represent the learning progression as students move from the *Uncovering Student Ideas* formative assessment probe to the *explore-before-explain* activities. Each model lesson vignette also includes an explanation, ways to evaluate student learning, and possible elaborations to extend the learning.

SAFETY IN ELEMENTARY SCIENCE

It is important to implement safety practices within the context of science investigations, whether this is in a traditional classroom, laboratory, or in the field. When you keep safety in mind up front as a teacher, you avoid many potential issues with the lesson while also protecting your students. Teachers should be aware of and support any school or district safety policies, legal safety standards, and better professional practices that are in place, and investigations should apply those safety protocols that align with the work being conducted in the lesson.

Safety practices encompass things considered in the typical science classroom (e.g., wearing safety goggles or safety glasses with side shields, vinyl gloves, and nonlatex aprons as appropriate), while other focus areas such as engineering require that students can demonstrate how to use equipment before allowing their use. Science investigations should always be supervised and safety procedures should be reviewed prior to initiating any hands-on activities or demonstration. Each of the lessons within this module includes teacher guidelines for applicable safety procedures that should be followed. For each investigation, teachers should remind student teams specifically what the safety procedures are that they should follow.

Information about classroom science safety, including a safety checklist for science classrooms, general lab safety recommendations, and links to other science safety resources, is available at the Council of State Science Supervisors website at CSS-Science.org/safety.shtml. The National Science Teaching Association (NSTA) provides a list of science rules and regulations, including standard operating procedures for lab safety and a safety acknowledgment form for students and parents or guardians to sign. You can access

Table 2. *Template with Design Questions for Teachers*

Stage 1: Identify Evidence-Based Claim
Establish Exploratory Experience (Firsthand) • What evidence-based experience will students have that allows them to construct a scientific claim? **Materials:** **Procedures:** • What procedural explanations might you need to explain? (Not mini content explanations.) **Safety:**
Establish Content (Minds-On) • What content will students make a claim about that will serve as the context for science learning?
Stage 2: Creating Conceptual Coherence
Pinpoint *Uncovering Student Ideas* Formative Assessment Probe That Hooks Learning • How can you motivate students and captivate their attention using science phenomena or culturally relevant life experiences? • What specific ideas or misconceptions can you preassess during the Engage phase? • What are the content-based learning targets for the lesson? • What scientific practices are learning targets for the lesson?
Use Explanations to Enhance Learning • What underlying principles do you need to help students formulate? • What terms and concepts do you need to introduce that are essential for understanding? • What other terms or ideas that are related to the content are considered nice to know or nonessential topics, or will be important in another unit?
Provide Transferring Practice • What firsthand investigation can students have to test an idea in a new situation or build a new idea in a similar situation?
Include Growth Indicators for Students and Teachers • How will students think about their developing knowledge? • What assessment will be used to determine whether students have gained the necessary abilities and knowledge?

the safety acknowledgment form for elementary students at https://static.nsta.org/pdfs/Safety AcknowledgmentForm-ElementarySchool.pdf. In addition, NSTA's Safety in the Science Classroom web page (NSTA.org/safety) has numerous links to safety resources, including safety papers written by the NSTA Safety Advisory Board.

Disclaimer: The safety precautions of each activity are based in part on use of the recommended materials and instructions, legal safety standards, and better professional practices. Selection of alternative materials or procedures for these activities may jeopardize the level of safety and therefore is at the user's own risk. Additional information regarding safety procedures can be found on other NSTA sites, including the NSTA Safety Portal: Safety in the Science Classroom.

REFERENCES

Ericsson, K. A., N. Charlness, P. J. Feltovich, and R. R. Hoffman, eds. 2006. *The Cambridge handbook of expertise and expert performance.* Cambridge: Cambridge University Press.

National Research Council (NRC). 2012. *A framework for K–12 science education: Practices, crosscutting concepts, and core ideas.* Washington, DC: National Academies Press.

1

EXPLORING
"Magnets in Water"

INTRODUCTION TO THE LESSON

In this lesson, elementary students **explore** how different materials interact with magnets and **explain** how magnetism is a noncontact force depending on the materials involved. The lesson begins by engaging students' initial ideas about whether magnets need materials to work. It then provides students with firsthand experiences essential for understanding how magnetic forces can act at a distance and close by and be understood by exploring patterns demonstrated when magnetic objects contact each other and other materials.

MATERIALS NEEDED FOR THIS LESSON

- "Magnets in Water" formative assessment probe (included)

- Paper clips

- Transparent containers, such as cups, beakers, or Tupperware

- Magnets, such as a bar magnets, wand magnets, or other magnets that could be used to test classroom materials. (*Safety note:* Do not use neodymium magnets, also known as super magnets or power magnets. These are powerful and can injure the user if handled incorrectly!)

- Various metals such as a brass clip, iron nail, steel washer or piece of wire, copper penny, silver coin, nickel, small piece of tin, square of aluminum foil, or zinc-coated nail. (*Safety note:* Do not

use objects made of lead, which is a hazardous material.)

SAFETY NOTES

1. Have direct adult supervision while you are working with magnets.

2. Use caution when working with sharp items such as pushpins and nails, which can puncture or scrape the skin.

3. Wear safety glasses with side shields or safety goggles during the setup, hands-on, and takedown segments of the activity.

4. Use caution when working with glassware (e.g., glass beaker), which can shatter if dropped and cut or puncture skin.

5. Immediately wipe up any spilled water or other items on the floor so they do not become a slip-and-fall or trip-and-fall hazard.

6. Use caution in handling magnets near each other. Fingers and skin can get caught between strong magnets and can injure hands.

7. Keep magnets away from your mouth! They can be hazardous if swallowed.

8. Wash your hands with soap and water after completing this activity.

Magnets in Water

Four friends were wondering if magnets could pick up steel paper clips in water. This is what they said:

Nate: "I think magnets and paper clips need to be in air. If both the magnets and paper clips are in water, they won't attract."

Amy: "I think magnets need to be in the air, but it doesn't matter if the paper clips are. Magnets can attract paper clips covered with water."

Steve: "I don't think air makes a difference. I think magnets will attract paper clips when both are underwater."

Leah: "I don't think air makes a difference. However, when magnets are in water, they work the opposite way. The paper clips will be repelled by the magnet."

Which friend do you agree with and why? Explain your thinking about how magnets work.

_____

_____

_____

_____

_____

_____

_____

_____

"MAGNETS IN WATER" PROBE BACKGROUND INFORMATION

Teacher Explanation

The best answer is Steve's: "I don't think air makes a difference. I think magnets will attract paper clips when both are underwater." Magnetism is a force that can work through a gas, a liquid, and even a solid (e.g., nonmagnetic materials such as paper, wood, aluminum foil, tape, and plastic). Just as electricity moves through some materials better than others, magnetism moves with ease through some materials and has more difficulty passing through other materials. Although most people's experiences with magnets happen in an environment where the magnet is surrounded by air, magnets also work underwater and in other gaseous environments, such as carbon dioxide or helium. Magnets also work in environments without an atmosphere or air. For example, a magnet on the Moon or a magnet in a bell jar with all the air removed will attract iron objects.

Research on Students' Ideas Related to This Probe

- Research has shown that some students are inclined to link gravity with magnetism (Driver et al. 1994). If they believe gravity is necessary for magnets to work and also believe that gravity has no or less of an effect underwater, they may believe magnets will not attract objects in the water.

- Barrow (1987) investigated students' awareness of magnets and magnetism across age ranges and found that they were aware of magnets through their everyday experiences of sticking objects to refrigerators with magnets. However, before instruction, few students could explain magnetism, especially in terms of forces and how magnets work (Driver et al. 1994).

- Bar and Zinn (1989) sampled 98 students ages 9–14 and found that 40% believed that a medium (air) was necessary for magnets to affect objects.

THREE-DIMENSIONAL LEARNING TARGETS FROM A FRAMEWORK FOR K–12 SCIENCE EDUCATION

Disciplinary Core Idea: *Grades 3–5:* Types of Interactions: Electric, magnetic, and gravitational forces between a pair of objects do not require that the objects be in contact—for example, magnets push or pull at a distance. The sizes of the forces in each situation depend on the properties of the objects and their distances apart and, for forces between two magnets, on their orientation relative to each other.

Scientific Practices: Investigating Questions, Planning and Carrying Out Investigations, Constructing Scientific Explanations

Crosscutting Concept: Patterns

CONNECTIONS BETWEEN THE FRAMEWORK, FORMATIVE ASSESSMENT PROBE, AND EXPLORE-BEFORE-EXPLAIN LESSON

Before students connect that magnetism is a force that exists between two objects that do not have to be in contact, they first **explore** and **explain** how magnets and objects such as metal paper clips interact with one another in water and the types of materials that are magnetic. The "Magnets in Water" formative assessment probe elicits students' initial ideas about how magnets work and engages their interest in exploring magnetic properties. The probe provides teachers with information on commonly held student ideas that are challenged during the lesson. As students gather data from their **exploration**, they look for patterns to help them revise and construct an **explanation** of how magnets work. With teacher guidance, students develop more sophisticated understanding of magnetic forces and the properties of magnetic materials. At the end of the lesson, students revisit the probe and revise their initial claims. Students use patterns they notice in data as evidence from their investigations and their conceptual understanding of how magnetic forces work.

VIGNETTE: EXPLORING "MAGNETS IN WATER"

The lesson started with the "Magnets in Water" probe to find out whether students believed magnets would work in water (Keeley and Tugel 2009, pp. 67–72). The probe also helped students consider whether magnets and objects attracted to magnets have to touch for a magnetic interaction. The lesson began with students selecting the best answer choice that matched their prediction. Table 1.1 shows the range of initial ideas students had about magnetic interaction in air and water. While a little over half of the students (58%) held correct conceptions of how magnetic forces travel through air and water, 42% of them held inaccurate ideas. The initial use of the probe generated a list of class ideas. This step is essential so that all students can see that their ideas are acknowledged, that not everyone has the same idea, and that they need to work together to figure out the best answer and explanation for the phenomenon of using magnets in water.

After making and sharing their predictions, teams of two students received magnets (magnetic wands) to test the ideas generated by the class. First, they tested Amy's answer by observing

Table 1.1. *Student Responses to "Magnets in Water" Formative Assessment Probe*

Selected Response Items	Student Responses (n = 36)	Representative Written Explanations of Student Thinking
Nate: "I think magnets and paper clips need to be in air. If both the magnets and the paper clips are in water, they won't attract."	11% (4)	"They don't attract if something is between them."
Amy: "I think magnets need to be in the air, but it doesn't matter if the paper clip is. Magnets can attract paper clips covered with water."	6% (2)	"I think if a magnet is in water, it will not work."
Steve: "I don't think air makes a difference. I think magnets will attract paper clips when both are underwater."	58% (21)	"Magnets don't work any different in water. It's just like having it out of water. It will attract."
Leah: "I don't think air makes a difference. However, when magnets are in water, they work the opposite way. The paper clips will be repelled by the magnet."	25% (9)	"I think that if both the magnet and paper clips are underwater, they will repel instead of attracting." "I think the water will make the magnet push away the paper clip."

Source: Keeley and Tugel (2009, p. 67).

whether magnetism works when the paper clip is in water and the magnet is in air. Each pair of students had a small, transparent plastic cup filled with water. They placed a paper clip in the water, and then tested whether they could move the paper clip with the magnet without submerging the magnet in water. Their observation revealed an interaction when the object was in the water but the magnet was in the air. This led to testing Steve's idea—that there would be an interaction when both the magnet and paper clip were underwater—by putting both objects into the water. Students observed an interaction. Using the evidence from this observation, they rejected Nate's idea that magnets won't attract if both objects are in the water. They also dismissed Leah's, since the evidence from their observation showed that the paper clip was attracted to the magnet, not repelled by it. The class then discarded Amy's idea, since their evidence showed that the magnet attracted the paper clip both when it was underwater and when it was in the air. Finally,

the class concluded that Steve's was the best answer and that magnetism passes through water and air, but they wondered whether it could pass through a solid material.

Building on their question to extend the probe, students were asked whether they thought they could move a paper clip with a magnet if they put various solid objects— a sheet of paper, a notebook, and the wooden tabletop—between the paper clip and the magnet. Next, students tested whether magnetism could pass through each of these items. This exploration led to students using evidence to describe how magnetism passes through various materials.

Now that students had discovered that magnetism is a force that can attract a metal paper clip in air, underwater, and even when some solid materials are placed between the magnet and the paper clip, the following exploration asked students to generate a list of objects in the science classroom they thought would or would not be attracted to a

Table 1.2. *Results of Formative Assessment Probe to Determine Students' Conceptions of Magnetic Materials*

Magnetic Items	Nonmagnetic Items	Representative "Rules" Students Used to Determine Whether an Object Was Magnetic
File cabinet drawer Staple Door handle Cabinet handle Spoon Paper clip Nail Pushpin	Cabinet Lab table Door Whiteboard Binder Pencil Felt Book Poster Wooden shelf Plastic chair Cup Floor Plastic trash can Tissue	"If the object can attract certain types of metal, it's magnetic." "If it looks metal, then it is magnetic, but if it looks like plastic or paper, then it is not magnetic." "If it has metal in it or is made of something magnetic, then it is magnetic." "To be magnetic, it must be copper, nickel, or zinc."

magnet and to state the rule that they used to make their decision (Table 1.2). In the previous exploration, students had observed how a metal paper clip attracted a magnet and how magnetism passed through nonmetallic materials. Using reasoning based on this evidence, they listed metal items in the classroom as magnetic and nonmetal items as nonmagnetic. Table 1.2 shows the cumulative lists of materials that students identified as being magnetic or nonmagnetic, as well as representative "rules" they used to determine whether an object was magnetic.

After completing the assessment, a whole-class discussion took place in which students made connections between certain materials and the list they had constructed. For instance, they noted that door and cabinet handles appeared to be made from the same types of metal. However, students could also identify that not all metal objects in the room contained the same type of metal and that a penny was made of a different metal than either the door or cabinet handles.

Next, students tested whether the classroom materials they had identified were magnetic. Finally, pairs of students used their magnets to investigate the materials they had listed as being magnetic or nonmagnetic. Once students had tested all the materials on their list, they were asked to revisit and revise, if necessary, the rule they used to determine whether materials are magnetic based on the data they had collected.

Explanation

The whole-group discussions focused on the data from the prior activities—the assessment probe and the exploration of magnetic and nonmagnetic materials. For example, one team noticed that magnetism could travel through the water and through the paper and the textbook but not through the wooden tabletop. A student suggested, "We need a more powerful magnet for it to travel through the thick tabletop." While students wanted to emphasize whether magnetism can travel through specific materials like water and paper, the probing questions asked them to think more broadly about whether magnets need to touch the object to work. For example, the focus on probing questions asked students to develop scientific explanations for phenomena by looking for patterns in data versus thinking about one specific incident. Thus, students could see a pattern that magnetism did not require materials to touch; however, they would need a stronger magnet to go through thicker materials such as the wooden tabletop.

In the classroom investigation of magnetic materials, the class returned to the data table on the front board and added a column to their predicted results (Table 1.1) headed "Actual Results." Then, as a class, students tallied the actual results. Students thought it was interesting that most metal objects, except a metal spoon and the door handle, were attracted to the magnet, while none of the nonmetal objects were attracted to the magnet. They began to revise their initial thoughts about magnets generated from our class list. In this way, they learned that the accumulation of data could help them revise and elaborate their evidence-based claims.

At this point in the lesson, it was time to discuss the big ideas as a whole group, and students were invited to explain what they knew about the properties of magnets. Students observed from the data they collected that not all metals are magnetic. As one student put it, "The metal in the spoon must be a type of metal that is not magnetic." This statement is valid and was a scientific claim the student made from evidence collected. Next, the class embarked on a quick test to help them understand which classroom metals were magnetic. The items they tested included a brass clip, iron nail, steel washer, piece of wire, copper penny, silver coin, nickel, small piece of tin, aluminum foil square, and zinc-coated nail. To the students' surprise, only two of these metal objects were magnetic: the iron nail and the steel washer.

Evaluation

Now that students could explain magnetic forces, they revisited the probe, making new claims supported with evidence from their **explorations** to construct a **scientific explanation** that included ideas about whether magnetism is a force that can push or pull objects without touching them. In addition, students were encouraged to use patterns in their data from their **explorations** to **explain** the types of materials that magnets would attract or repel.

Possible Further Elaborations

- Use additional formative assessment probes for elaboration experiences and checking on how well students can transfer the ideas from this lesson to other contexts. These can be found in the book *Uncovering Student Ideas in Physical Science, Volume 2: 39 New Electricity and Magnetism Formative Assessment Probes* (Keeley and Harrington 2014).

- Have students explore how they can make an object float using magnetism. For example, students might use magnetic rings that can be slid onto an acrylic rod mounted on a base or onto a handheld pencil. Have students predict how the rings can be arranged so that they appear to float with a small air space in between them. Ask students to connect their observation to a pushing or pulling force and whether contact between the objects is required.

REFERENCE

Bar, V., and B. Zinn. 1989. *Does a magnet act on the moon?* Scientific Report, The Amos de Shalit Teaching Centre. Jerusalem, Israel: Hebrew University.

Barrow, L. 1987. Magnet concepts and elementary students' misconceptions. In *Proceedings of the second international seminar on misconceptions and educational strategies in science and mathematics*, vol. 3, ed. J. Novak, 17–22. Ithaca, NY: Cornell University.

Driver, R., A. Squires, P. Rushworth, and V. Wood-Robinson. 1994. *Making sense of secondary science: Research into children's ideas.* London: Routledge.

Keeley, P., and R. Harrington. 2014. *Uncovering student ideas in physical science, Volume 2: 39 new electricity and magnetism formative assessment probes.* Arlington, VA: NSTA Press.

Keeley, P., and J. Tugel. 2009. *Uncovering student ideas in science, Volume 4: 25 new formative assessment probes.* Arlington, VA: NTSA Press.

2

EXPLORING
"Marble Roll"

INTRODUCTION TO THE LESSON

In this lesson, elementary students **explore** how changing the direction of a force allows them to **explain** the motion of an object. The lesson begins by eliciting students' ideas about the direction a marble will go after it exits a spiral track. It then provides data-based experiences that serve as evidence for students' thinking about how changing the direction of a force influences the resulting motion of a moving object. Students can manipulate forces to see the cause-and-effect relationship on the motion of an object.

MATERIALS NEEDED FOR THIS LESSON

- "Marble Roll" formative assessment probe (included)

- Track stand or another stand to replicate "Marble Roll" formative assessment probe

- Small steel ball bearing or marble

- ¾-inch-diameter plastic tubing or ½-inch foam pipe insulation that is approximately 3 meters long to create a track to test ball-bearing or marble motion

- Masking tape to secure track to different classroom structures, such as walls, desks, chairs, and bookshelves, or outdoors using the school's exterior walls, playground equipment, and trees

- Magnetic wand if steel ball bearing is used (this will allow students to move the ball bearing through the plastic tubing if it becomes stuck and can also stop the ball bearing at the end of the track)

- Reading: *Newton and Me* by Lynne Mayer (2010)

SAFETY NOTES

1. Have direct adult supervision while you are working with marbles.

2. Clear away all fragile items from the activity zone in case a moving marble becomes a projectile.

3. Wear safety glasses with side shields or safety goggles during the setup, hands-on, and takedown segments of the activity.

4. Quickly pick up any items used in this activity off the floor so they do not become a slip-and-fall or trip-and-fall hazard.

5. Keep marbles away from your mouth! They can be hazardous if swallowed.

6. Wash your hands with soap and water after completing this activity.

Marble Roll

Five friends built a marble tower. The marble tower had a curved track. The track was designed so that the marbles would move down the track in a circular path. The track ended on the floor. Each friend predicted how he or she thought the marble would move when it rolled off the end of the track onto the floor. This is what they said:

Magda: "I think it will roll in circles."

Soledad: "I think it will curve for a bit and then straighten out."

Allen: "I think it will roll in one big curve."

Keira: "I think it will roll in a straight line."

Rafael: "I think it will zigzag for a little while."

Which friend do you most agree with? _____

Use the picture above to draw the path you think the marble will take when it gets to the end of the track.

Explain your thinking. Why do you think the marble will move that way?

_____

_____

_____

_____

_____

_____

_____

"MARBLE ROLL" PROBE BACKGROUND INFORMATION

Teacher Explanation

The best answer is "straight." Students should draw a straight line. The marble will travel in a straight line when it leaves the track. As the marble rolls down the tower's spiral track, a force toward the center of the spiral (a centripetal force) caused by the outside wall of the track keeps the marble rolling in a spiral path. When the marble leaves the end of the track, it is no longer in contact with the track's walls. Without the track pushing on it, the marble no longer has a center-directed force acting on it that causes it to roll in a curved path. According to Newton's first law of motion, an object will remain at rest or in uniform motion in a straight line unless acted on by an outside force. Because there is no longer a center-directed force exerted by the wall of the track pushing on the marble, the marble rolls off the track and across the floor in a straight path. It will continue this way unless an outside force causes it to change direction or slow down and stop.

Research on Students' Ideas Related to This Probe

- Students often expect that objects moving in a curved path because of a wall or constraint will continue to do so when the wall or constraint is removed. This belief that the wall or constraint "trains" the object to follow a curved path is deeply rooted in students and persists even with targeted instruction in middle and high school (Arons 1997).

- Students have difficulty perceiving that the direction of motion will be in a straight line when they observe situations like an object set in motion inside a curved hollow tube (Gunstone and Watts 1985).

- Children need to develop the language tools to describe motion appropriately before understanding the principles (Driver et al. 1994).

THREE-DIMENSIONAL LEARNING TARGETS FROM *A FRAMEWORK FOR K–12 SCIENCE EDUCATION*

Disciplinary Core Idea: *Grades K–2:* Pushing or pulling on an object can change the speed or direction of its motion and can start or stop it. *Grades 3–5:* The patterns of an object's motion in various situations can be observed and measured; when past motion exhibits a regular pattern, future motion can be predicted from it.

Scientific Practices: Carrying Out Investigations, Analyzing and Interpreting Data, Constructing Scientific Explanations

Crosscutting Concepts: Patterns, Cause and Effect

CONNECTIONS BETWEEN THE *FRAMEWORK*, FORMATIVE ASSESSMENT PROBE, AND *EXPLORE-BEFORE-EXPLAIN* LESSON

Before students consider how interactions between forces and motion can be explained and predicted, they **explore** and **explain** how creating different kinds of tracks will influence a rolling marble's speed and direction. The "Marble Roll" formative assessment probe elicits children's predictions about the motion of an object and how they use motion words to describe the path of a moving object. It is extended in this lesson to develop ideas about the forces applied to a moving object and its resulting motion, such as how the direction of a force created by a spiral track influences the motion of marbles when they leave a track. The probe provides teachers with information on students' commonly held ideas about the relationships between the direction of a force and the resulting motion of an object and how to describe the direction of motion. As students gather data during their **explorations**, they learn that they can manipulate the direction of a push applied to influence the direction and speed of an object. Students' **explanations** directly result from their learning by noticing patterns and cause-and-effect relationships when they change a variable in a scientific investigation. With teacher guidance, students can begin to explain that many different factors influence the motion and speed of an object. At the end of the lesson, students revisit the probe and use their firsthand experiences to explain that the motion results from the direct force applied to the object.

VIGNETTE: EXPLORING "MARBLE ROLL"

The lesson started with the "Marble Roll" formative assessment probe, used to uncover students' prior knowledge and experiences and create a context for learning that would be the storyline for understanding concepts associated with forces and motion (Keeley 2013, pp. 71–74). Most students thought the marble would start on a curved path and eventually straighten out. As one put it, "I think it will do a loop because it is turning a bunch, so I think it will keep that motion" (see Figure 2.1). No students thought the marble would roll in either a straight line or a zigzag pattern after leaving the spiral track. Thus, the probe got students thinking about describing different motion patterns (e.g.,

straight, zigzagged, curved, round) and a causal relationship between changing the direction in which the force is applied and the resulting motion.

Students gathered around the setup as we performed the investigation with a steel ball bearing. One student dropped the ball bearing at the top of the track. Everyone watched what happened as the ball bearing traveled down the circular path. The room grew silent as students focused on the path the ball bearing took as it exited the track. Finally, nearly in unison, the students said out loud, "We were wrong, and it went in a straight line!" (For a video of the setup and results, visit YouTube.com/watch?v=xiz90syCVH8.)

The formative assessment probe affirmed to the class that our initial ideas are not always right, but that investigations can provide data that serve as evidence to help us answer scientific questions (*NGSS* Lead States 2013). The evidence came from students' observations of the marble leaving the track in a straight line, countering their initial ideas and creating a desire to figure out the phenomenon.

The next step in the exploration was to collect data about the different variables at play in a mar-

Figure 2.1. *Students' Ideas About the* Uncovering Student Ideas *Probe*

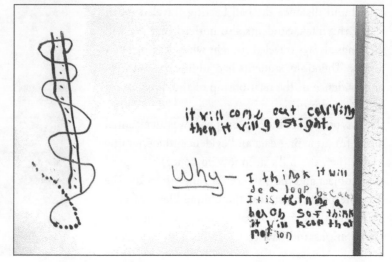

ble track. We started by exploring this investigative question: "How does changing the steepness of a hill influence the distance and speed at which a ball bearing travels?" Working in groups of three, student teams each made three user-controlled ramps that varied in steepness—slight hill, moderate hill, and steep hill—from a 3-meter-long section of clear tubing (the same kind used in the "Marble Roll" demonstration) and masking tape. Students used the classroom as the infrastructure for their tracks, which they taped to the walls, chairs, and desks. Each group also had magnetic wands to remove the ball bearings if they became stuck at any point on the track. Before letting their ball bearings run the three tracks, students predicted which one would allow the marble to travel the farthest and move the fastest.

Students' data were qualitative, and they inferred speed from what they witnessed as the ball bearing traveled down the different hills. To measure distance, students used masking tape to mark on the floor how far the ball bearing traveled when it left each of the tracks. Students noticed patterns in the data, such as that the ball bearings that went faster also traveled a farther distance across the floor. This simple learning by exploring helped students learn that the hill's steepness was directly related to the speed and distance the ball bearing traveled when it left the track. Students also noticed that the ball bearings always traveled straight when leaving their tracks. Therefore, students had additional confirming evidence of the relationship of the direction of a force and motion.

This portion of the Explore phase was an essential hook for attaching data and evidence to a scientific claim (i.e., the hill's steepness influences the speed of an object and the distance the object travels). The Explore phase illustrated the unique blend of content, practices, and logical thinking with students' observations and data comparisons across variables

(i.e., steepness of the hill). Thus, multiple data points served as evidence that aided their construction of scientific claims (*NGSS* Lead States 2013).

The second portion of the exploration used ideas in slightly new and different circumstances. For example, students were challenged to make a track where the ball bearing would go over one hill positioned in the middle of the track. Before testing, students were asked to make predictions based on prior experiences. Their first tests were unsuccessful for nearly half the students (see Figure 2.2). For example, as Riley explained, "My first hill was the right tallness, but then the second hill was too tall for the marble to climb." Students learned from this exploration that changing an object's motion requires a change in the direction of force applied to the object.

Figure 2.2. *Students' Unsuccessful Marble Track With Two Hills*

Because this was an iterative process, students could modify their designs to create a track that accomplished the task. However, before they were allowed to test their modified tracks, students were asked to explain their thinking for their modifications. Having students explain their thinking helps make the experience minds-on, and students actively engage in thinking through their ideas and developing understanding versus learning simply through trial and error. For example, most students explained that they could resolve their issues by creating a second hill that was less steep than their initial plan. Students realized that there was a direct causal relationship between the steepness of the two hills. The initial hill needed to be steep enough for the ball bearing to reach the top of the first hill and continue to move over the second hill.

Explanation

The explanation phase started with a read-aloud of *Newton and Me* (Mayer 2010). The class frequently stopped and talked through this story of a boy and his dog, Newton, to develop ideas about the factors that influence forces and motion in our daily lives. For example, the book supported students in developing a conceptual understanding that the strength of a push or pull influences motion. In addition, the reading related to what students knew about how the surface might influence the motion and speed of an object (frictional forces). For example, students considered why a ball rolls farther on a smooth surface in a carpeted room than on the grass outside (pp. 4–5). The reading was also a way to introduce formal science vocabulary that related to students' firsthand experiences, and they learned that "pushing and pulling are forces of motion" (Mayer 2010, p. 26).

The idea from the reading that pushing creates a force was then applied to students' experiences during the "Marble Roll" probe. With teacher guidance, the class considered what was pushing the marble as it traveled down the track. As the marble traveled, the track pushed the marble. The sides of the track pushed the marble in a circular path when the track was arranged in a spiral. When the marble came off the track, there was no longer a force pushing it in a circular direction, and therefore, the marble went straight.

Evaluation

The students revisited the "Marble Roll" formative assessment probe to explain why a marble travels in a straight line when it leaves a spiral track. In addition, the teacher guidance provided during the explanation helped students describe how the shape of the track influenced the direction in which the marble was pushed. Students justified in their scientific explanation that the marble travels in the direction in which "it is being pushed," which is directly caused by the track. At the end of the track, the marble "goes straight out" because that is how the "track points." Students were prompted to use arrows in their explanations to model the direction of force and the resulting motion of the object.

Possible Further Elaborations

• Challenge students to make tracks with one loop or other, more complicated designs. Suggested probing questions include asking students to predict how the marble will travel at different points on the track. Students can model the direction of forces created by the track and the direction of motion using arrows. Have students draw models of the direction of forces before moving a marble through the track. Ask students whether the direction of their force arrows matched the direction the marble traveled.

REFERENCES

Arons, A. 1997. *Teaching introductory physics.* New York: John Wiley and Sons.

Driver, R., A. Squires, P. Rushworth, and V. Wood-Robinson. 1994. *Making sense of secondary science: Research into children's ideas.* London: Routledge.

Gunstone, R., and M. Watts. 1985. Force and motion. In *Children's ideas in science,* ed. R. Driver, E. Guesne, and A. Tiberghien, 85–104. Milton Keynes, UK: Open University Press.

Keeley, P. 2013. *Uncovering student ideas in primary science: 25 new formative assessment probes for grades K–2.* Arlington, VA: NTSA Press.

Mayer, L. 2010. *Newton and me.* Mount Pleasant, SC: Arbordale.

NGSS Lead States. 2013. *Next Generation Science Standards: For states, by states.* Washington, DC: National Academies Press. NextGenScience. org/next-generation-science-standards.

3

EXPLORING
"Needs of Seeds"

INTRODUCTION TO THE LESSON

In this lesson, elementary students **explore** how different factors influence seed germination and **explain** the factors required for seeds to sprout. The lesson begins by engaging students' initial ideas about what factors are necessary for seeds to sprout. It then provides students with firsthand experiences collecting data on how seeds have specific requirements to germinate.

MATERIALS NEEDED FOR THIS LESSON

- "Needs of Seeds" formative assessment probe (included)

- Containers with separate compartments, such as ice cube trays or egg cartons

- Fast-sprouting seeds, such as radish seeds (if seed packets are not available, dried beans from the supermarket can be substituted). (*Safety note*: Use only pesticide-free seeds.)

- Eyedroppers

- Goggles

- Soil

- Aluminum foil

- Small paper cups

- Magnifying glasses

- Reading: *Rosie Sprout's Time to Shine* by Wortche (2011)

SAFETY NOTES

1. Have direct adult supervision while you are working with seeds and soil.

2. Wear safety goggles and nonlatex aprons during the setup, hands-on, and takedown segments of the activity.

3. Quickly pick up any items used in this activity off the floor so they do not become a slip-and-fall or trip-and-fall hazard.

4. Keep seeds away from your mouth! They can be hazardous if swallowed.

5. Make sure mold or mildew does not grow on the soil, as they can cause allergic reactions in some students.

6. Wash your hands with soap and water after completing this activity.

Needs of Seeds

Seeds sprout and eventually grow into young plants called *seedlings*. Put an X next to the things you think most seeds need in order to sprout.

___ water

___ soil

___ air

___ food

___ sunlight

___ darkness

___ warm temperature

___ Earth's gravity

___ fertilizer

Explain your thinking. Describe the "rule" or reasoning you used to decide what a seed needs in order to sprout.

_____

_____

_____

_____

_____

_____

_____

_____

_____

"NEEDS OF SEEDS" PROBE BACKGROUND INFORMATION

Teacher Explanation

The best response is that seeds need water, air, food, and warmth. Like all living things, the plant embryo inside a seed needs these four ingredients to carry out the life processes that support its germination and growth. The young plant embryo needs food as its source of energy and building material for growth, but the food it needs is already contained within the seed in the form of a cotyledon, since a young sprout does not yet have the leaves to carry out photosynthesis. Air is necessary for seeds to respire. Seeds must take in oxygen to use and release energy from their food. Seeds also require a warm temperature and water for the life-sustaining chemical reactions that take place in the cells of the young plant embryo to occur. However, some seeds, such as acorns, need to go through a cold period before they germinate. Too much water can "drown" seeds by preventing them from taking in oxygen and causing them to rot. Some seeds can sprout in humid air without the need for a moist surface. Hence, the right amount of water needs to be available.

Seeds can sprout without soil as long as they have a source of moisture. Sunlight is not needed, as evidenced by the fact that many seeds germinate when covered by soil. Gravity affects the ability of the sprout to send its early root structures downward, but seeds can sprout even in conditions where gravity is much less than that on Earth. Seeds have sprouted in microgravity in space. Seeds do not need fertilizers; these are used by plants once they have established roots and can take in substances from the soil to provide essential elements to the cells that make up the plant structures.

Research on Students' Ideas Related to This Probe

- Many children think that plants always need light to grow, and they apply this idea to germination (Driver et al. 1994).

- Some students fail to recognize a seed as a living thing; therefore, they do not recognize that seeds have needs similar to those of other living things (Driver et al. 1994).

- Students appear to believe that food and light are necessary for all stages of plant growth. They often do not understand that while light is a requirement for food making, it is not required for growth. A study conducted by Roth, Smith, and Anderson (1983) found that students held firmly to the idea that plants always require light, even in the face of contrary evidence, such as observing seedlings germinating in the dark (Driver et al. 1994).

- Russell and Watt (1990) interviewed 60 younger students about their ideas on growth conditions, focusing on germination and vegetative growth. Ninety percent of these students identified water as necessary. Only a few mentioned air, gases, food (which to them meant soil nutrients), sun, light, or heat (Driver et al. 1994).

- Some students have difficulty distinguishing between germination and vegetative growth (Driver et al. 1994).

THREE-DIMENSIONAL LEARNING TARGETS FROM A *FRAMEWORK FOR K–12 SCIENCE EDUCATION*

Disciplinary Core Idea: *Grades K–2*: Germination, life cycles, needs of organisms, seeds. Plants need to take in water and light to grow. *Grades 3–5*: Plants have external structures that support survival, growth, and reproduction.

Scientific Practices: Analyzing and Interpreting, Carrying Out Investigations, Constructing Explanations

Crosscutting Concepts: Patterns, Cause and Effect

CONNECTIONS BETWEEN THE *FRAMEWORK,* FORMATIVE ASSESSMENT PROBE, AND *EXPLORE-BEFORE-EXPLAIN* LESSON

Before students consider how plant structures serve various functions to support growth and survival and what plants need to grow, they begin with the seed and what it needs to start the plant's growth process through germination. They **explore** and **explain** how different factors influence the germination of a seed into a seedling. The "Needs of Seeds" probe elicits students' incoming ideas about plants, engages their interest in exploring what is necessary for seeds to sprout, and provides teachers with information on commonly held ideas. As students gather data from their **explorations,** they look for patterns and cause-and-effect relationships to construct and revise an **explanation** of the factors that seeds need to sprout and those that affect the growth of the sprouted seeds (seedlings). Then, with teacher guidance, students learn terms for specialized plant structures observed during their exploration. At the end of the lesson, students revisit the probe and revise their initial claims using crosscutting concepts of patterns and cause and effect to construct a scientific explanation with evidence from their investigations about the needs of seeds.

VIGNETTE: EXPLORING "NEEDS OF SEEDS"

Students started the Engage phase with the "Needs of Seeds" formative assessment probe (Keeley, Eberle, and Tugel 2007, pp. 101–6). Nearly all students thought that seeds needed sunlight, soil, and water to grow. Students were torn on whether seeds needed warmth, food, and fertilizer. Grades K–2 students did not know enough about gravity to speculate on this factor. Students focused on their past experiences planting seeds and growing flowers versus clarifying why certain variables in the probe were essential for a seed to sprout and grow into a seedling. Charlie explained, "Because they need water and soil or they cannot grow." Students set out to test many different variables in the "Needs of Seeds" formative probe with ideas in mind.

Students were excited to learn that we would be directly testing their ideas. Working in pairs, they used ice cube trays and egg cartons as planters. Each well in the container could be used for a separate test, and they could do additional test trials. They also had radish seeds, water, and soil. They could easily use the setup to test whether seeds need light. To collect data on sunlight, they would place aluminum foil over certain variables in our exploration. The pairs of students would use their containers to start the investigation.

As a class, students were walked through the investigation setup. The materials were in front of the groups and placed on butcher paper to make the experience less messy. Each pair of students shared an ice cube tray, although both students performed the same tests. Students also received small magnifying glasses for closer inspection. Each group received a bag of soil with a small cup to apply soil for certain test conditions. First, each student put soil in two wells (four total in each container, since they worked in pairs). While students were careful to place soil in the wells, some spillover into other wells was inevitable. Students used a paper towel to remove excess or misplaced soil onto the butcher paper gently. Next, students practiced how to use the eyedropper to add water to their different tests.

After practicing with the eyedropper, they started setting up the trials. First, each student used the experimental setup in Box 3.1 using the following materials: radish seeds, soil, water, and foil. Then they used eyedroppers to add water to the wells (see Figures 3.1 and 3.2). Placing the seeds under aluminum foil was to test whether radish seeds needed light to grow. The class did not test fertilizer or gravity. With the experiment set up, it was time for students to record their first data point. They had a

sheet with a grid that represented our testing setup. Students drew and labeled how they set up their investigation.

A teacher demonstration was created using the same setup and placed in the refrigerator to see if temperature influenced seed germination. The teacher demonstration container would be pulled out each day so students could observe the influence of temperature on germination. The test results were quick to come in. After only three days, students started to see the cause-and-effect relationship between variables and seed germination. Students excitedly shouted out, "It's happening!" A closer look with magnifying glasses showed the first

Box 3.1. *Summary of Experimental Setup*

Students work in pairs and use ice cube trays as their planters. Each well in the container can be used for a separate test. Each group receives a bag of soil (or all students can share from a common source) to test specific conditions. In addition, each group receives a cup of water and an eyedropper. Teachers may need to practice using the eyedropper to add water. Finally, students need several radish seeds (two per well being tested).

1. Each student puts soil in two wells (four total in each container, since students work in pairs). Next, students add two radish seeds underneath the soil in these wells. This test is to see if seeds germinate with soil and no water.

2. Each student places water in two of the container wells and puts two radish seeds in each well. This test is to see if seeds germinate with water and no soil.

3. Each student puts soil in two more wells, then adds two radish seeds underneath the soil in each well. Have students add water to the soil until it is damp. This test is to see if seeds need soil and water to grow.

4. Each student places two radish seeds in an empty well. Students do nothing to these seeds. This is a test of whether seeds will germinate on their own.

5. Completely cover four small paper cups with foil. To collect data on sunlight, students place the small disposable cups wrapped in aluminum foil over one each of the seeds in the soil, the seeds in water, the seeds in wet soil, and the seeds in an empty well. This test is to see if light is necessary for each of the conditions for seed germination.

specks of yellowish-green coloring in the sprouted seeds with water (see Figures 3.3a and 3.3b).

Next, students were challenged to take a closer look at the seed on its own (just light) and the one in soil with no water. To students' surprise, they observed no evidence of green or any other indicators that the seed had changed. Next, students carefully removed the foil to see what was happening to the seeds in the dark conditions. Some students noticed that the seed with water had also sprouted, while the other seeds showed no change. Students drew their observations of the sprouted seed (seedling) and labeled their pictures. They also observed the teacher's demonstration of the investigative setup that had been placed in the cold refrigerator. The teacher's demonstration was anticlimactic, with the seeds showing no evidence of sprouting.

The excitement grew over days four through six, as students noticed changes in seedling growth. All students observed little yellow stems and tiny yellowish-green leaves sprouting from the seedlings in water. These seedling changes occurred in both light and dark conditions (see Figure 3.4). As students crowded around their seedlings, they made qualitative observations and drew their seedlings' development.

The seedlings were now growing taller than the container, so students had to slightly change the procedure at this point. Instead of placing the foil back over the wells, students wrapped empty paper cups with foil, and then placed these

over the same wells to test whether plants grow in darkness (see Figure 3.5).

After five days, students still saw no evidence of seedling development or growth in the other conditions: the seeds on their own, with no water or soil, and the seeds in soil with no water, in both dark and light conditions, did not grow. In addition, the teacher's demonstration with seeds in the cold treatment was revealed each day, but there was no sign of growth.

Figure 3.1. *Setting Up the Test Conditions Using an Egg Carton*

Figure 3.2. *Placing Foil Over Some Seeds to Simulate Germinating Seeds in Dark Conditions*

Figure 3.3a and 3.3b. *Students' First Observation of Seed Germination*

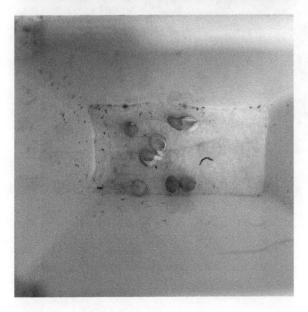

Explanation

To hook content on students' evidence-based claims, students gathered in a circle and participated in a read-aloud of *Rosie Sprout's Time to Shine* (Wortche 2011). To help them connect the reading with their experiences in class, they discussed clarifying questions about the narrative and pictures. When the book talked about plants needing light, soil, and water to grow, students considered whether and how what the book said was similar to or different from their experiences with seeds and seedlings. Aiden noted, "Our plants did not need soil or light to grow, and only water." The book used many of the same words as students had in class, such as *seed, root, stem,* and *sprout*. These terms introduced the idea that plants have different parts that help them survive and grow. Students enjoyed how Rosie took daily measurements, much as we had in class. At the end of the story, students discussed their favorite characters. Students liked Rosie's story because "she was a good friend" and "took good care of her plant."

Evaluation

Now that students could explain some essential germination and seedling growth requirements, they revisited the probe, making new claims supported by their explorations. Students revised their initial ideas and constructed an evidence-based claim about what seeds need to sprout that included the factors we had tested. Students were also encouraged to draw pictures of plants and their parts and use words like *seeds, water, roots, soil,* and *sunlight* to explain what the young plants (seedlings) need to grow. Students were also able to describe similarities and differences between the needs of seeds and the needs of the seedlings using the same factors listed in the probe. They needed to recognize that the disciplinary core idea that a plant needs sunlight to grow applies to the seedling, but not to a plant's seed.

Possible Further Elaborations

- Students can continue to use their sprouting seedlings to conduct further tests using the same variables (water, soil, light versus darkness). In addition, students can explore how structures like roots, stems, and leaves change over time.

- "Seeds in a Bag" is a related probe that focuses on seeds' need for water and whether students recognize that the water has to be taken in by the seed (Keeley 2013).

REFERENCES

Driver, R., A. Squires, P. Rushworth, and V. Wood-Robinson. 1994. *Making sense of secondary science: Research into children's ideas*. London: Routledge.

Keeley, P. 2013. *Uncovering student ideas in primary science: 25 new formative assessment probes for grades K–2*. Arlington, VA: NTSA Press.

Keeley, P., F. Eberle, and J. Tugel. 2007. *Uncovering student ideas in science, Volume 2: 25 more formative assessment probes*. Arlington, VA: NSTA Press.

Roth, K., E. Smith, and C. Anderson. 1983. *Students' conceptions of photosynthesis and food for plants*. East Lansing: Michigan State University, Institute for Research on Teaching.

Figure 3.4. *Students' Observation of Seedling Growth in Both Light and Dark Conditions*

Figure 3.5. *Students' New Experimental Design to Collect Data on Seedling Growth in Both Light and Dark Conditions*

Russell, T., and D. Watt. 1990. *SPACE research report: Growth*. Liverpool: Liverpool University Press.

Wortche, A. 2011. *Rosie Sprout's time to shine*. New York: Random House Children's Books.

4

EXPLORING
"Sink or Float?"

INTRODUCTION TO THE LESSON

In this lesson, elementary students **explore** whether the shape of an object determines if it will sink or float. By changing the shape of an object and measuring its weight and size, they can explain that sinking and floating depend on multiple observable properties. This lesson is designed to help students connect the physical properties of materials with how they affect the way an object functions.

MATERIALS NEEDED FOR THIS LESSON

- "Sink or Float?" formative assessment probe (included)
- Small baby pool or 25- to 50-gallon container for whole-class activities
- Small containers for individual and pair activities
- Modeling clay
- Steel objects, such as a paper clip, spoon, and wrench
- Picture of a steel-hulled tanker or cargo ship

SAFETY NOTES

1. Have direct adult supervision while you are working on this activity.

2. Wear safety goggles and nonlatex aprons during the setup, hands-on, and takedown segments of the activity.

3. Quickly wipe up spilled or splashed water off the floor so it does not become a slip-and-fall hazard.

4. Keep water-filled baby pool away from electrical receptacles to prevent accidental shock.

5. Use caution when working with clay. Use only moist clay. Dried-out clay or clay dust may contain silica, which is a health hazard.

6. Wash your hands with soap and water after completing this activity.

Sink or Float?

Circle the person with the best idea.

What are you thinking?

"SINK OR FLOAT?" PROBE BACKGROUND INFORMATION

Teacher Explanation

Bonita has the best answer: "I think sometimes clay sinks and sometimes it floats." Clay is denser than water. Therefore, by itself, clay sinks whether it is formed in the shape of a ball, pencil, or pancake. However, clay can be flattened and the sides turned up into a boatlike form. This shape now contains two materials—clay and a volume of air (like an empty cup or boat)—allowing the clay to float. The mass-to-volume ratio (density) of the shape containing clay and air is less than the mass-to-volume ratio of a clay shape not containing air. This explanation is for adult learners, however; the focus for K–2 should be on the change in shape, not the mass-to-volume ratio. Students in grades 3–5 can begin making quantitative measurements of the object's weight, volume, and size.

Research on Students' Ideas Related to This Probe

- Students' ways of looking at floating and sinking include the roles played by material, weight, shape, and water (Driver et al. 1994).

- A study conducted by Biddulph and Osborne (1984) asked students ages 7 to 14 why things float. The typical response was "because they are light."

- Some students use an intuitive rule of "More A–More B" (Stavy and Tirosh 2000). They reason that if you have a larger object (a bigger piece of clay), it must sink, while a smaller piece will float.

- Children younger than age 5 typically ignore an object's size and focus on its "felt weight" (Smith, Carey, and Wiser 1984).

THREE-DIMENSIONAL LEARNING TARGETS FROM A FRAMEWORK FOR K–12 SCIENCE EDUCATION

Disciplinary Core Ideas: Grades K–2: Matter can be described and classified by its observable properties (e.g., visual, aural, textural), by its uses, and by whether it occurs naturally or is manufactured. *K–2 Engineering*: Develop a simple sketch, drawing, or physical model to illustrate how the shape of an object helps it function as needed to solve a problem.

Scientific Practices: Developing Models, Carrying Out Investigations, Analyzing and Interpreting Data, Constructing Scientific Explanations

Crosscutting Concepts: Patterns, Cause and Effect, Structure and Function

CONNECTIONS BETWEEN THE FRAMEWORK, FORMATIVE ASSESSMENT PROBE, AND EXPLORE-BEFORE-EXPLAIN LESSON

Before elementary students start to think about the multiple physical factors that influence an object's mass-to-volume ratio, they **explore** and **explain** how shape and size influence whether an object sinks or floats. The "Sink or Float?" formative assessment probe elicits primary students' ideas on and past experiences with how the shape of an object influences whether it will sink or float. The probe provides teachers with ideas about students' prior knowledge that will be confronted during the lesson. As students collect data during their **explorations**, they notice patterns in the measured weight of the clay for the three shapes of clay tested and whether each shape sinks or floats. Students' **explanations** are directly based on patterns they notice in their data related to the shape of an object, its weight, and whether it floats or sinks.

Using the data as evidence helps students explain that neither an object's weight alone nor its shape alone determines whether it sinks or floats. Instead, with teacher guidance, students start to realize that myriad factors influence whether an object sinks or floats.

VIGNETTE: EXPLORING "SINK OR FLOAT?"

The lesson started with the *Uncovering Student Ideas* probe "Sink or Float?" (Keeley 2013, pp. 45–48). The probe asks students to consider three different student ideas about whether clay floats or sinks. Students' ideas represented the persistence of beliefs about sinking and floating being related to the shape and size of an object. Most students (91%) agreed with the argument presented by Bonita and thought that "sometimes clay sinks and sometimes

Figure 4.1. *Students' Belief That Shape Influences Floating and Sinking*

Figure 4.2. *One Student's Belief That Whether the Clay Is Soft or Hard Influences Floating or Sinking*

it floats," depending on whether the clay is flattened like a pancake (see Figure 4.1). One student thought it was less about the shape and whether the clay was soft or hardened (see Figure 4.2). Only a few students (9%) thought it would sink regardless of the shape.

Before testing whether different shapes influence sinking or floating, students created the three shapes illustrated in the *Uncovering Student Ideas* probe: round ball, rolled pencil, and flat pancake. They used the same amount each time and weighed the clay. All students found that the clay had the same weight regardless of its shape. Since all students received the same small amount of clay, their weight measurements were similar, approximately 3.7 grams (see Figures 4.3–4.5).

The class headed outside and used a small baby pool to test the probe. First, all students tested a

Figures 4.3–4.5. *Clay in Different Shapes, Round, Pencil-like, and Pancake-like, All Having the Same Weight*

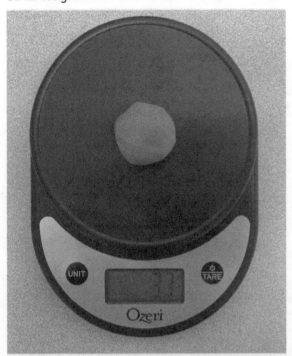

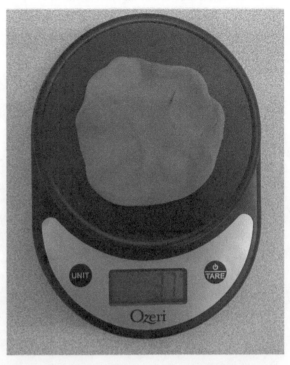

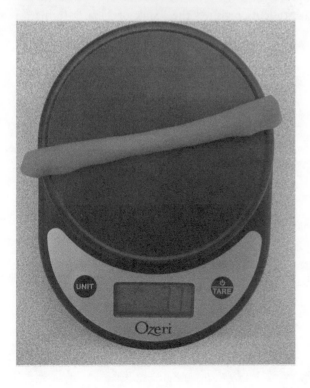

clay ball, which sank. Next, they stretched and rolled their clay into a pencil-like shape and placed it in the water. The pencil-shaped clay sank as well. Finally, students flattened their clay into a pancake shape. To their surprise, and contrary to their prediction, this clay also sank. (See teacher video resource at https://youtu.be/WlqD_1qJovo.)

Next, students set out to explore whether the properties of other materials influence whether they sink or float. The goal was to have students compare properties like size, weight, and shape to understand what makes objects made of certain materials float or sink. For this exploration, all students received different-sized objects made of steel, such as a paper clip, a spoon, and a wrench. They predicted whether the object's weight would affect whether it would sink or float. For example, the students predicted that the spoon and wrench would sink because they were "heavy for their size" but thought the paper clip might float. They tested the objects and found that all three sank.

The teacher then showed them a picture of a large cargo ship with a steel hull and asked them to think about how it could float even though it was made out of the same material as the steel objects they had just tested. How was the boat's shape different from the clay shapes and steel objects they had previously tested? Could they create a model of a boat using the clay to show how a material that sinks can be made to float? Students were asked to first draw their models of clay boats and then test their models using the clay. They weighed the clay so that they used the same amount of clay as in the other tests, changing only the shape. The students discovered that turning up the sides of the flattened clay allowed it to float. The teacher then asked them to sink their floating clay boats and observe whether they floated back up. The students observed that even though they had changed the shape so the boat could float, the same shape could also sink.

Explanation

In the explanation phase, students displayed what they had learned during the different sinking and floating investigations. They made some overarching scientific claims based on data they used as evidence for sensemaking. First, they noticed a pattern in the clay weight data. Next, students used multiple individual data points as evidence to claim that (1) weight does not change when we alter an object's shape and (2) weight alone does not determine whether an object sinks or floats. Finally, they connected what they had observed with their clay boats to how a steel tanker ship can float.

Next, students needed to learn that shape alone does not determine whether an object sinks or floats. The students were puzzled at how the same shape that floated when the sides were turned up

like a boat could also be made to sink. The teacher pressed them to consider the difference between the floating clay boat shape and the same shape that sank. The students came up with the idea that when the boat was floating, it had air in it, but when water got inside the boat, that made it heavier, causing it to sink. The other objects that sank were not shaped so they could hold air. Therefore, the shape made a difference when it allowed the object to be filled with a lighter material such as air. There was a cause-and-effect relationship between the shape and the material: If the shape could hold air, the material could be made to float.

Finally, of the four shapes of clay tested, students could explain why three sank and one floated. With teacher guidance, students began to conceptualize whether an object sinks or floats as influenced by the combination of observable physical properties such as shape, size, weight, and material.

Evaluation

Students revisited the "Sink or Float?" formative assessment probe to explain how shape can determine whether an object sinks or floats. Students supported their **scientific explanations** with both quantitative (weight) and qualitative (description of the object's shape) data and whether the material sank or floated. Students were prompted to think beyond the formative assessment probe and consider the importance of conducting comparisons to solve an engineering problem, such as making something float out of a material that sinks. It helped students see how engineering is similar to science in that, like science, it also uses evidence from data.

Possible Further Elaborations

- An additional probe that can be used to further *explore-before-explain* or formatively check students' understanding of the relationship between size and whether an object floats or sinks is "Watermelon and Grape" (Keeley 2013, Model Lesson 5 in this book).

- Have students make aluminum foil boats to hold cargo, such as pennies, snap blocks, or other objects of the same size and weight. What shape allows the boat to hold the heaviest cargo?

REFERENCES

Biddulph, F., and R. Osborne. 1984. Pupils' ideas about floating and sinking. Paper presented at the Australian Science Education Research Association Conference, Melbourne.

Driver, R., A. Squires, P. Rushworth, and V. Wood-Robinson. 1994. *Making sense of secondary science: Research into children's ideas.* London: Routledge.

Keeley, P. 2013. *Uncovering student ideas in primary science: 25 new formative assessment probes for grades K–2.* Arlington, VA: NTSA Press.

Smith, C., S. Carey, and M. Wiser. 1984. A case study of the development of size, weight, and density. *Cognition* 21 (3): 177–237.

Stavy, R., and D. Tirosh. 2000. *How students (mis) understand science and mathematics: Intuitive rules.* New York: Teachers College Press.

5

EXPLORING
"Watermelon and Grape"

INTRODUCTION TO THE LESSON

In this lesson, elementary students **explore** the size and weight of everyday materials and **explain** how whether an object is heavy or light for its size determines if it sinks or floats. The lesson starts by engaging and eliciting students' ideas about whether they think a watermelon and a grape will sink or float. It then provides students with experiences in making observations of the sizes and shapes of objects to describe the physical properties of materials.

MATERIALS NEEDED FOR THIS LESSON

- "Watermelon and Grape" formative assessment probe (included)
- 10-gallon fish tank
- Eight gallons of water
- Watermelon
- Grape
- Various objects to compare and contrast, such as different-sized fruits (e.g., cranberries and a pumpkin) and other items like a marble and a weight

SAFETY NOTES

1. Have direct adult supervision while you are working on this activity.

2. Wear safety goggles and nonlatex aprons during the setup, hands-on, and takedown segments of the activity.

3. Quickly wipe up spilled or splashed water off the floor so it does not become a slip-and-fall hazard.

4. Keep water-filled aquarium away from electrical receptacles to prevent accidental shock.

5. Do not taste or eat food used in this activity.

6. Wash your hands with soap and water after completing this activity.

Watermelon and Grape

The watermelon will sink.	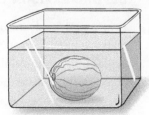	**The grape will sink.**	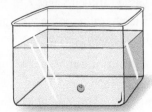
The watermelon will float.		**The grape will float.**	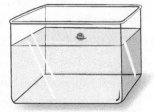

What are you thinking?

"WATERMELON AND GRAPE" PROBE BACKGROUND INFORMATION

Teacher Explanation

"The watermelon will float" and "The grape will sink" are the best answers. Although the watermelon is much larger than the grape and its felt weight is much greater, its mass-to-volume ratio (density) is less than that of a grape. Also, its density is less than that of water; therefore, it floats. The grape's mass-to-volume ratio is greater than the watermelon's even though its felt weight is much less. The density of a grape is greater than that of water; therefore, it sinks. Denser objects are heavy for their size, while less-dense objects are light for their size. An object denser than water sinks; an object less dense than water floats. Thus, it is the mass-to-volume ratio that makes a difference, not the size.

Research on Students' Ideas Related to This Probe

- A study conducted by Biddulph and Osborne (1984) asked students ages 7 to 14 why things float. The typical response was "because they are light."

- Some students use an intuitive rule of "More A–More B" (Stavy and Tirosh 2000). They reason that the larger an object the more likely it is to sink.

- Children younger than age 5 typically ignore an object's size and focus on its felt weight (Smith, Carey, and Wiser 1984).

- Piaget's studies (1973) demonstrated that children initially think of a pebble as being "light" and later describe it as "light for them" but "heavy for water." He showed that when children reach ages 9 and 10, they begin to relate the density of one material to that of another material by describing some materials

as floating because they are lighter than water (Driver et al. 1994).

THREE-DIMENSIONAL LEARNING TARGETS FROM A FRAMEWORK FOR K–12 SCIENCE EDUCATION

Disciplinary Core Idea: Grades K–2: Matter can be described and classified by its observable properties (e.g., visual, aural, textural), by its uses, and by whether it occurs naturally or is manufactured.

Scientific Practices: Carrying Out Investigations, Analyzing and Interpreting Data, Constructing Scientific Explanations

Crosscutting Concepts: Patterns, Scale, Proportion, and Quantity

CONNECTIONS BETWEEN THE *FRAMEWORK*, FORMATIVE ASSESSMENT PROBE, AND *EXPLORE-BEFORE-EXPLAIN* LESSON

Before students learn how to describe materials by their measurable properties, they first **explore** and **explain** using multiple observations to describe objects. The "Watermelon and Grape" formative assessment probe elicits students' ideas on and past experiences with whether objects sink or float depending on size. The probe provides teachers with information about common misconceptions that will be challenged during the lesson. As students collect data from their **explorations**, they notice patterns in an object's felt **heaviness** and **size** and whether it sinks or floats. Next, students circle back to test whether additional objects sink or float. Finally, they begin to formulate how the "heavy or light for its size" property of an object influences whether it sinks or floats. Students' **explanations** are a direct consequence of their firsthand experiences. With teacher guidance, students can develop a more profound concept of physical properties, including many different observations considered in tandem. At the end of the lesson, students revisit the formative assessment probe to explain that sinking and floating are based on an object's weight in relation to its size.

VIGNETTE: EXPLORING "WATERMELON AND GRAPE"

The lesson started with the *Uncovering Student Ideas* probe "Watermelon and Grape" (Keeley 2013, pp. 49–52). The probe specifically asks students whether they think a watermelon and a grape will sink or float. The ideas were attractive to students, and nearly all thought the watermelon would sink and the grape would float. When asked to explain their thinking, students' responses focused on using the object's weight to determine whether it would sink or float. For example, Harry explained, "The watermelon will sink because it's heavy." Interestingly, one student thought the watermelon would float and the grape would sink. Logan said, "I picked the watermelon will float because it has air inside and the grape does not because it is small" (see Figure 5.1).

Thus, Logan based his prediction on thinking about the materials inside a watermelon versus a grape. The probe's purpose was to elicit student ideas about sinking and floating and see whether they could substitute a prediction with a rule for their thinking. Therefore, engagement time was not about the correctness of students' ideas, but rather how they logically supported their predictions. The probe revealed a research-identified commonly held intuitive rule, known as "More A–More B," in which students reason if there is more of one thing, then there is more of another. For example, if an

Figure 5.1. *Student's Idea About Why a Watermelon and a Grape Will Sink or Float*

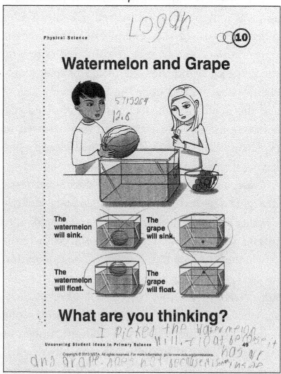

object has more weight or a greater size, students believe that it is more likely to sink.

Next, with ideas in mind, it was time for students to explore whether the watermelon and grape would sink or float. We performed the investigation as a classroom demonstration using a 10-gallon fish tank. (See the teacher video resource at https://youtu.be/L_Pc6sxB_gI). First, the grape was placed in the tank. To the students' surprise, the grape sank and went straight to the bottom of the tank. Next, we placed the watermelon in the tank. Most students were shocked when the watermelon did not sink to the bottom. However, they were torn on whether the watermelon was sinking or floating. They associated floating with being completely suspended on top of the water, although they could see water between the watermelon and the bottom of the fish tank. For example, Harry noticed that the watermelon did not sink to the bottom and was only partially submerged. Described a bit differently, half of the watermelon was below the water's surface. Students were perplexed as to why the grape sank and the watermelon floated. Harry claimed that he had done the investigation before and this is not what he had found. Thus, students' conceptions were persistent, and they resorted to explanations that justified their initial ideas despite having data as evidence to the contrary.

Next, we set out to do some additional tests. The goal was less about having students identify whether objects would float or sink and geared more toward having them think about objects in terms of whether they are heavy or light. The exploration focused on the idea that weight and size alone do not determine whether objects sink or float. First, students extended the formative assessment probe and compared other fruits, including cranberries and a pumpkin. They compared the relative heaviness of the objects, and then predicted whether each would sink or float based on what they had learned from the "Watermelon and Grape" investigation. Students closely compared the grape and cranberry. While nearly the same size and similar in shape, many thought the cranberry would float because it was "lighter." Students were less sure about comparing the pumpkin and watermelon but believed they felt the same and commented that the pumpkin should float like the watermelon. Then students watched the demonstration and saw that the pumpkin floated like the watermelon. Thus, the experience added further evidence that weight alone does not determine whether an object sinks or floats.

Further objects were added to the students' investigation, including a small marble, weight, and water balloon. Students immediately thought both the marble and weight would sink, basing their explanation on a difference between these materials and the fruits tested. They believed that these objects did not have water in them and thus would sink. Students' conceptions were verified, as both the marble and weight sank. Students were less sure about the water balloon. Most thought it would sink because the water balloon felt heavy. Some students thought the water balloon would be suspended in the middle of the tank because, as they explained, "it was water just like the water in the tank."

Explanation

The Explain phase began with students' evidence-based claims described during class discussions. They had two similar experiences that served as evidence for their claims. First, students consolidated their data into two categories, one on each half of their sheet, with the headings "Heavy for its size" and "Light for its size." Next, they drew pictures of each item tested and listed whether it would sink or float under one of the headings. Students made the following evidence-based claims: First, an object's weight alone does not determine whether it sinks or floats. Students could support this claim with the watermelon and pumpkin versus the grape and cranberry. Second, shape on its own does not explain whether an object sinks or floats. Students' claims were supported with evidence that even similar-shaped objects like apples, avocados, and tomatoes differ in whether they sink or float. With teacher guidance, students began to explain sinking and floating as related to both the size and shape of an object. Aiden explained that a "small object that feels heavy will sink like a small rock." While students could do most of the evaluation activity independently, they needed help in regard to the watermelon and pumpkin. All students thought these two objects were heavy and did not have a frame of reference for whether they were heavy for their size. Still, Charlie remarked that even "really big objects can float if they are really big in size as the watermelon."

Thus, students were starting to think about heaviness in a relative sense and realizing that not all objects perceived to be heavy float in water. The culminating activity allowed students to see patterns across the different experiences as evidence that shape and size do not determine whether objects sink or float. Having students summarize all their experiences on one sheet allowed them to understand the similarities among the various floating and sinking experiences.

Evaluation

Students revisited the "Watermelon and Grape" formative assessment probe to explain that size and shape determine whether an object sinks or floats. Students were able to support their **scientific explanation** with evidence that small objects that are heavy for their size, like a grape, will sink and large objects that are light for their size, like a watermelon, can float. Encourage students to think using relative comparisons, as they need a frame of reference for considering whether an object is heavy or light for its size. While students revised their claims, they were prompted to think about sinking and floating based on observations such as size, shape, and materials that make up the object rather than just one factor alone.

Possible Further Elaborations

- Have students predict and explain whether a tiny piece of material will sink or float versus a large piece of material. You might demonstrate with a tiny speck of soap versus a bar of whole soap, for example. (Do not use Ivory soap, which floats!)

- Have students test materials that are more porous, like a sponge or a cube with holes in it, to extend their thinking about how air and space might affect sinking and floating.

- An additional probe that can be used to further *explore-before-explain* or formatively check students' understanding is "Sink or Float?" (Keeley 2013, Model Lesson 4 in this book).

REFERENCES

Biddulph, F., and R. Osborne. 1984. Pupil's ideas about floating and sinking. Paper presented at the Australian Science Education Research Association Conference, Melbourne.

Driver, R., A. Squires, P. Rushworth, and V. Wood-Robinson. 1994. *Making sense of secondary science: Research into children's ideas.* London: Routledge.

Keeley, P. 2013. *Uncovering student ideas in primary science: 25 new formative assessment probes for grades K–2.* Arlington, VA: NTSA Press.

Piaget, J. 1973. *The child's conception of the world.* London: Paladin.

Smith, C., S. Carey, and M. Wiser. 1984. *A case study of the development of size, weight, and density. Cognition* 21 (3): 177–237.

Stavy, R., and D. Tirosh. 2000. *How students (mis) understand science and mathematics: Intuitive rules.* New York: Teachers College Press.

6

EXPLORING
"Shadow Size"

INTRODUCTION TO THE LESSON

In this lesson, elementary students explore how some materials allow light to pass through and explain how shadows are created. The lesson begins by engaging students' incoming ideas about shadow size. It then provides data-based experiences in which students create shadows using different materials as evidence for explaining that some materials allow light to pass through them, while others do not. Students learn how they can change the shape and size of a shadow depending on how they position the light source.

MATERIALS NEEDED FOR THIS LESSON

- "Shadow Size" formative assessment probe (included)
- Small handheld flashlight
- Objects of different shapes and colors, such as both solid and translucent blocks (plastic toy animals or other figures also work well in the explorations)

- White surface, such as a white poster board or science fair display board for each student (alternatively, you might have students perform their investigations directly on a white or light-colored wall in the classroom or hallway)
- Reading: *What Makes a Shadow?* by Clyde Bulla (1994)

SAFETY NOTES

1. Have direct adult supervision while you are working on this activity.

2. Use caution when moving in the area if lights are dimmed for this activity in case of trip-and-fall hazards.

3. Wash your hands with soap and water after completing this activity.

Shadow Size

How can you make the shadow bigger?

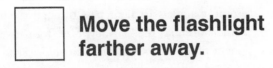

☐ **Move the flashlight closer.**

☐ **Move the flashlight farther away.**

☐ **It doesn't matter. The shadow stays the same.**

What are you thinking?

"SHADOW SIZE" PROBE BACKGROUND INFORMATION

Teacher Explanation

The best answer is "Move the flashlight closer." The smaller the distance between a light source and an object, the larger the shadow; the larger the distance between a light source and an object, the smaller the shadow.

Research on Students' Ideas Related to This Probe

- Students' preconceptions about shadows come from their everyday personal experiences, which may vary from student to student. These preconceptions based on experiences can put learning constraints on students' development of an understanding of light and shadows (Barrows 2012).

- Studies by Neal, Smith, and Johnson (1990) showed that some students do not connect shadows with a light source. Other students consider a shadow as being pushed out by the light. The researchers also found that some students think the size of a shadow is based on the size of the object.

- Some students view shadows as objects rather than understanding that shadows are created when light is blocked. Conceptual development is required for students to understand the relationship between a light source, an object, and the shadow cast by the object. Working with flashlights can give children an opportunity to directly challenge their everyday conceptions about shadows, providing them with powerful early experiences in scientific ways of knowing (Magnusson and Palincsar 2005).

THREE-DIMENSIONAL LEARNING TARGETS FROM A *FRAMEWORK FOR K–12 SCIENCE EDUCATION*

Disciplinary Core Idea: *Grades K–2*: Some materials allow light to pass through them, others allow only some light through, and others block all the light and create a dark shadow on any surface beyond them, where the light cannot reach. (Boundary: The idea that light travels from place to place is developed through experiences with light sources, mirrors, and shadows, but no attempt is made to discuss the speed of light.)

Scientific Practices: Carrying Out Investigations, Analyzing and Interpreting Data, Constructing Scientific Explanations

Crosscutting Concepts: Patterns, Cause and Effect

CONNECTIONS BETWEEN THE *FRAMEWORK*, FORMATIVE ASSESSMENT PROBE, AND *EXPLORE-BEFORE-EXPLAIN* LESSON

Before students make connections between the transfer of light and objects not in contact with each other, they first **explore** and **explain** how shadows are created and can change shape and how some materials let light pass through them, while others do not. The "Shadow Size" formative assessment probe elicits students' initial ideas and creates a need-to-know situation about how shadows can change size depending on the position of the light source. The probe provides teachers with information on students' commonly held ideas that will be challenged during the lesson. As students gather data from their **explorations**, they notice patterns in the materials that create shadows and a causal relationship between the size of the shadow created and the distance from the light source. Students' **explanations** are a direct result of learning by creating shadows. With teacher guidance, students can explain that light transfers from the source (the flashlight) to the object, and then to the wall, creating a shadow of the object. The shadow is an area with less light than the surroundings. At the end of the lesson, students revisit the probe and use crosscutting concepts of patterns and cause-and-effect relationships they observe in the data to explain the role of the materials in letting light pass through them and the position of the light source in creating a shadow.

VIGNETTE: EXPLORING "SHADOW SIZE"

The purpose of the Engage phase was to elicit students' ideas and situate the learning context. Students started the lesson with the *Uncovering Student Ideas* probe "Shadow Size" (Keeley 2013, pp. 79–82). Students all thought they needed to move the flashlight closer to make a shadow bigger. Interestingly, they reasoned that "objects faraway look smaller so the shadow will be smaller." Students had basic ideas about creating shadows, so they were challenged to change how the shadow appears.

The Explore phase of the formative assessment probe was designed to set the context for exploring shadows. Students worked in groups of two to build a tower of solid blocks of different shapes, sizes, and colors (see Figure 6.1).

Once students had built their towers, it was time for them to explore shadows. Students eagerly showed how to move their flashlights closer to their structures to make larger shadows and farther away to make smaller shadows. In this way, students quickly learned a cause-and-effect relationship. As Charlie explained, the closer his light was to the object, "the bigger the darkness." Asking *what*, *why*, *how* questions and having the students use descriptive words (e.g., in front of, behind, larger, smaller) during this time helps foster reflection about the relationship between the position of the light source, the structures, and the shadows created. In addition, students benefit from clarifying questions about how a shadow might look different when the flashlight is pointed directly at the tower versus at an angle to the structure. (The teacher modeled pointing the flashlight directly at a tower versus at an angle.) Finally, the teacher repeatedly referred to

Figure 6.1. *Students' Towers Built out of Different-Colored Blocks*

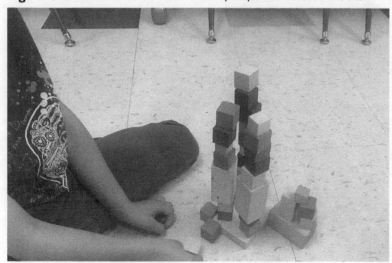

the darkness and black areas as shadows to encourage students' use of scientific vocabulary.

Through their exploration, students learned how the shadows differed when they pointed the light source directly versus indirectly at their structures. For instance, a pair exchanged the following observations when they aimed the flashlight at a triangular block:

Lennon: "If I shine the light right at it, the shadow is the same."

Finley: "Watch this: When I shine it over here [aiming the light at an angle], I can make it really pointy."

Thus, students learned that pointing the light source directly at an object creates a shadow that is identical to the object, while pointing the light source indirectly can cause shadows to stretch (see Figure 6.2).

The students were eager to explore independently, and many learned they could position two lights at different angles to create more than one shadow of the object. In Skyler's words to her partner with a second flashlight, "Point your light over here [at a different angle] and we can make two [shadows] appear when there is really just one [object]." Next, they experimented with positioning their flashlights at various angles all around their structures to make shadows. Depending on their flashlight positioning, some shadows stretched farther and were more distorted than others. Finally, nearly all students pointed their flashlights directly at the whiteboards and realized they did not create shadows. At this point, assessments were based on students' verbal and scientific ideas about the light sources and shadows created.

Next, students explored additional investigative questions about their structures and shadows. First, the class thought about the colored blocks they used in their towers and the shadows created. Many students noticed an immediate similarity between the shadows made by different-colored blocks. "The shadow is always black," one child said, pointing to

Figure 6.2. *Exploring the Shadows Created by Different-Colored Solid Blocks and Transluscent Objects*

the shadow made by the light on a structure containing red blocks. Another child suggested, "All blocks make a black shadow." Students' conversations assessed their developing knowledge of the shadows created by different materials.

Students were also supplied with transparent shapes to add to their structures. They were asked to predict what they thought would happen when they shone their lights on the translucent shapes. Most students thought they would "see through them" because they could "look through them." While students had initial ideas, many were surprised by what they observed when shining their lights on their structures. Students noticed an immediate pattern in the images formed by solid versus translucent shapes. First, as Avery excitedly explained, "The light on the wall is green like the rectangle." Thus, students learned that a light shining on a translucent material creates an image of the same color as the object. Second, students noticed patterns across the data. For example, solid objects create black shadows, while translucent materials create shapes the same color as the object.

Explanation

Following the students' explorations and evidenced-based claims, they engaged in a read-aloud of *What Makes a Shadow?* (Bulla 1994). Each page contains pictures and explanations, allowing students to confirm their developing knowledge and attach scientific vocabulary to conceptual understanding. Students were directed to think of the shadow as the absence of light ("no light in the area"). As the reading continued, the text became a springboard for discussions and opportunities for students to reflect on their firsthand experiences. Students stopped and thought about making shadows with their hands bigger and smaller based on the light source's position (pp. 24–26). Students resonated with these

ideas, as Dakota recalled making a shadow of a dog using his hand and a flashlight, and Charlie recounted that as long as you have a light source, you can create shadows in dark rooms. The students were excited to use their new ideas to make shadows at home. The reading served to provide students with another source of knowledge to verify their evidence-based experiences and promoted more elaborated understanding that built on and extended their learning. The book had the added benefit of promoting English language arts learning related to learning and understanding from informational texts (CCSS.ELA-Literacy.R1.K.1–10).

Evaluation

Students revisited the "Shadow Size" formative assessment probe to explain how to make a shadow larger. They justified their **scientific explanations** that a closer light source creates a larger shadow with data from their **explorations**. Students were encouraged to draw a model to illustrate the causal relationship between the light source and shadow created.

Possible Further Elaborations

- Have students test their understanding of shadows using irregular-shaped objects. For example, you might add a small plastic toy animal to the objects they use to make shadows and ask them to predict what will happen when they shine a light on the animal. Will the animal create a dark shadow or a colorful image?

- Share how shadow puppets have been used in India and China for over a thousand years. Then ask students to explain how they could use evidence from their investigation to create a shadow puppet show.

REFERENCES

Barrows, L. 2012. Helping students construct understanding about shadows. *Journal of Education and Learning* 1 (2): 188–191.

Bulla, C. R. 1994. *What makes a shadow?* New York: HarperCollins.

Keeley, P. 2013. *Uncovering student ideas in primary science: 25 new formative assessment probes for grades K–2*. Arlington, VA: NTSA Press.

Magnusson, S., and A. Palincsar. 2005. Teaching to promote the development of scientific knowledge and reasoning about light at the elementary school level. In *How students learn science in the classroom*, ed. S. Donovan and J. Bransford, 421–469. Washington, DC: National Academies Press.

Neal, D., D. Smith, and V. Johnson. 1990. Implementing conceptual change teaching in primary science. *Elementary School Journal* 91: 109–131.

7

EXPLORING

"Do the Waves Move the Boat?"

INTRODUCTION TO THE LESSON

In this lesson, elementary students **explore** how water waves move and **explain** that waves have repeated patterns of motion that move through the water but do not move the water itself. This lesson begins by engaging students' ideas about whether waves move objects in the water. It then provides data-based experiences in which students create different waves for explaining wave parts and how waves travel.

MATERIALS NEEDED FOR THIS LESSON

- "Do the Waves Move the Boat?" formative assessment probe (included)

- Medium-size transparent plastic container that can hold at least 64 ounces of water

- Cork or bobber (any object that will float on water)

- Water

SAFETY NOTES

1. Have direct adult supervision while you are working on this activity.

2. Wear safety goggles and nonlatex aprons during the setup, hands-on, and takedown segments of the activity.

3. Quickly wipe up spilled or splashed water off the floor so it does not become a slip-and-fall hazard.

4. Keep water-filled container away from electrical receptacles to prevent accidental shock.

5. Wash your hands with soap and water after completing this activity.

Do the Waves Move the Boat?

☐ **Yes, the boat moves with the waves.**

☐ **No, the boat does not move with the waves.**

What are you thinking?

"DO THE WAVES MOVE THE BOAT?" PROBE BACKGROUND INFORMATION

Teacher Explanation

The best answer is "No, the boat does not move with the waves." A wave is a pattern of motion resulting from a disturbance that travels through a medium from one location to another. In this case, the medium is the water. The waves moves through the water (medium), but when they are moving across the surface of deep water, the water does not move with the waves. In other words, the waves do not carry the water (with the boat on it) toward the shore. A wave transports energy and does so without transporting matter in the direction it is moving. If you were to observe the boat on a lake, you would notice that it gently bobs up and down as the waves pass by it. The boat stays in about the same position and is not carried toward the shore because the water it is floating on is not transported by the waves. An analogy would be people in a football stadium doing the wave. The wave travels around the stadium, but the people stay in their seats and do not move with the wave.

Research on Students' Ideas Related to This Probe

- Informal interviews with young children during the field test of this probe indicated they thought that waves moved objects and a boat moved on a wave. However, be aware that students confused this idea with surfers and riding waves at the beach.

THREE-DIMENSIONAL LEARNING TARGETS FROM A FRAMEWORK FOR K–12 SCIENCE EDUCATION

Disciplinary Core Idea: *Grades 3–5:* Waves, which are regular patterns of motion, can be made in

water by disturbing the surface. When waves move across the surface of deep water, the water goes up and down in place; it does not move in the direction of the wave—observe, for example, a bobbing cork or seabird—except when the water meets the beach. (*Note*: This DCI was originally listed in the K–2 grade band endpoints in the *Framework*. The *NGSS* committee moved it to the grade 3–5 span because young children have difficulty grasping this idea. With careful instruction that focuses on the patterns of movement, this probe and lesson can be used with primary grade children.)

Scientific Practices: Developing and Using a Model, Carrying Out Investigations, Analyzing and Interpreting Data, Constructing Scientific Explanations

Crosscutting Concepts: Patterns, Cause and Effect

CONNECTIONS BETWEEN THE *FRAMEWORK*, FORMATIVE ASSESSMENT PROBE, AND *EXPLORE-BEFORE-EXPLAIN* LESSON

Before students connect how waves transfer energy, they first **explore** and **explain** how waves are created and move in water without the overall displacement of a floating object. The "Do the Waves Move the Boat?" formative assessment probe elicits students' initial ideas about waves and activates their interest in **exploring** how waves are created and move through the water. The probe provides teachers with information on commonly held student ideas that will be confronted during the lesson. As students collect data from their **explorations**, they notice patterns and cause-and-effect relationships and refine their **explanations** of how waves travel. With teacher guidance, students create drawings to show how waves go up and down in a repeating pattern but do not move a floating object in the direction of the wave. Students revisit the probe at the end of the lesson to revise their initial ideas and use crosscutting concepts to provide an evidence-based claim about how waves move through a medium like water but do not move the boat.

VIGNETTE: EXPLORING "DO THE WAVES MOVE THE BOAT?"

The purpose of the Engage phase was to elicit students' ideas and situate learning around the movement of waves. Students considered the formative assessment probe "Do the Waves Move the Boat?" (Keeley 2013, pp. 75–78). When students were asked to explain their thinking, many cited past experiences swimming, being in a canoe in the ocean, or seeing waves at a large lake. For example, Charlie claimed that "big waves would knock us down and cause us to move towards the shore." Aiden said that the waves would move a "floatie" to the shore. Briar thought, "The waves are moving and that pushes you" (see Figure 7.1).

Students had a flurry of ideas about waves that became apparent as they talked with their partners. Some students said they picked "Yes, the boat moves with the waves" but wanted to be able to choose "Maybe" because a big wave would sink the boat. The conversation also demonstrated that students had limited conceptions of what a wave represents, and most of their responses focused on what happens when the water meets the beach. So, they were asked to describe a wave. Students focused on the crashing down of water after it had reached its high point versus being a repeated pattern of motion. Students' ideas indicated that many of them had background experiences with waves but limited conceptions of waves in a scientific sense. With students' ideas engaged, it was time to explore the characteristics of waves and try to answer the *Uncovering Student Ideas* probe.

The exploration phase was about testing the probe's ideas and using data as evidence for sensemaking. Students worked in groups of two, and each pair was supplied with a large, deep plastic container, a cork, and water to explore how waves influence a floating object's motion. Meanwhile, the teacher modeled the procedure they would follow using a 10-gallon fish tank in front of the class. Students were told to roll up their sleeves and grab a pencil. They were to make a series of waves by moving their pencils straight up and down to see how the waves influenced how the cork moved on the water. On the count of three, one student from each team practiced making water waves by just moving the pencil up and down. After a short practice, their partners took a turn at making water waves.

Next, students would conduct multiple tests while carefully watching the motion of the cork. The first test would create water waves by moving

Figure 7.1. *Student Explanation of Their Thinking*

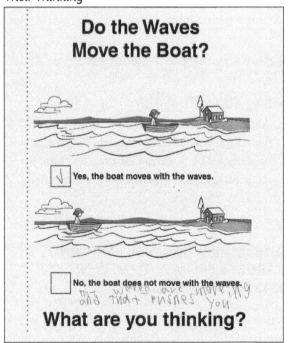

their pencils up and down approximately 10 cm away from the cork every 3 seconds. As students made water waves at this distance and frequency, they quickly noticed that the cork went up and down but did not go side to side or move in the direction of the waves they created. Charlie excitedly exclaimed, "Water waves don't move a boat and we were wrong," but Finley said, "Bigger waves would move the boat." The other partners tested this idea by forcefully moving the pencil up and down in the water 5 cm from the cork. The results were mixed, which led to a classroom debate. Some students' corks still went up and down, with the only difference being that the cork rose and fell a greater distance on the surface of the water. Other students were able to get the cork to move in the direction of the wave but were no longer correctly following the procedure, as they were moving the water side to side in the container.

Everyone was called to the front demonstration table so that students would not create false ideas related to what we were testing. By exaggerating how to carry out the procedure on the cork's movement, the teacher displayed the importance of creating an up-and-down versus side-to-side disturbance. Morgan said, "You are moving the pencil side to side, which is not what we are supposed to do." The demonstration showed that the forcefulness with which water waves are created changes the height of the waves but not whether they would move the cork across the water's surface.

Next, students explored the frequency of waves. They carried out a similar procedure but now created waves at regular intervals of 1 second. Starting with one partner from each team, student positioned their pencils approximately 10 cm from the cork. Each second, the teacher called out the word "wave" to tell students to dip their pencils in the water. Then their partners did the same thing with their pencils approximately 5 cm from the cork.

Once everyone had finished, they were asked to draw a wave in their science notebooks.

The explorations gave students multiple meaningful experiences to increase sensemaking. First, they showed students that water waves move an object up and down unless the water is pushed side to side. Second, the explorations broadened their ideas about waves. Students' drawings revealed that they conceptualized waves as patterns of repeated high and low points. These drawings contrasted with students' earlier ideas that a wave was just the crashing down of water after its high point because they illustrated their waves traveling across their plastic water containers. Finally, students' exploration experiences provided multiple pieces of data that served as evidence that while some waves may be more significant than others, they all have similar patterns and regular shapes. The students' evidence-based claims would be used to introduce scientific terminology during the Explain phase.

Explanation

Following the students' explorations and evidenced-based claims, they engaged in a read-aloud of *Waves: Physical Science for Kids* (Diehn 2018). There were specific parts of the book for students to focus on and connect to their firsthand experiences. The first essential ties between the book and students' explorations came early in the reading. For example, the following text reinforced students' firsthand experiences: "If you float on your back in a pond, do the waves move you to shore? After a long time, they might. But water in a wave isn't moving across the pond. Water in a wave is moving up and down, up and down" (Diehn, 2018, p. 4). Next, the class paused on the "Try This" question and reflected on how a foam ball would move in a bucket of water. Again, students drew on their firsthand experiences in the exploration to claim that the foam ball would move up and down but not side to side.

The reading also provided critical explanations of underlying principles that are not readily observable through direct exploration. For example, students learned that "waves happen because of energy. … When you see waves in water, it's the energy that's moving toward the shore, not the water" (Diehn 2018, p. 5). As the reading continued, the illustrations and text helped students develop more sophisticated understanding, and they observed drawings of waves similar to theirs, showing a repeated pattern (p. 6). Students acted out the book's description of "giant" waves that people make with their bodies during a baseball game (p. 8). Then they considered how the waves they created using their bodies were like the water waves. One student observed, "We went up and down like the water waves." Morgan tied an explanation to energy, saying, "We passed the wave along the classroom to move energy from each of us."

Evaluation

Now that students could explain that waves are a repeated pattern of motion that moves through water but does not move the water itself, they revisited the formative probe. Students revised their initial ideas and created **scientific explanations** based on their firsthand experiences during the **exploration**. Students were encouraged to draw wave models showing the repeated patterns of motion to support their explanations and to use crosscutting concepts of patterns and cause-and-effect relationships to illustrate how the forcefulness used to create a wave directly influences the height of the wave. Similarly, students used the concept of cause-and-effect relationships to show how repeatedly disturbing water's surface creates waves.

Possible Further Elaborations

- Have students create waves using string. They can tie one end of a string to a fixed point, and then hold the other end of the string to create a wave. Put a small bead on the string so students can practice making waves that move the bead up and down but not back and forth. Alternatively, have students make waves using the PhET simulation "Wave on a String" at https://phet.colorado.edu/sims/html/wave-on-a-string/latest/wave-on-a-string_en.html. Students can visualize a wave's repeated pattern of motion and how the wave moves through the string. Have students use their data to explain that the bead on the string moves up and down but not in the direction of the wave.

- Have students test other ways that might be used to move boats in deep bodies of water. Suggested investigations include making boats out of everyday materials and using handheld fans so students can move their boats on the water. Students can modify their boats to move at certain speeds across the water through an iterative engineering design process. Have students use their data to explain one way in which boats can move on water.

REFERENCES

Diehn, A. 2018. *Waves: Physical science for kids.* White River Junction, VT: Nomad Press.

Keeley, P. 2013. *Uncovering student ideas in primary science: 25 new formative assessment probes for grades K–2.* Arlington, VA: NTSA Press.

8

EXPLORING
"Batteries, Bulbs, and Wires"

INTRODUCTION TO THE LESSON

In this lesson, elementary students **explore** how to light a bulb using wires and a battery and **explain** how electrical energy transfers in a circuit. The lesson starts by eliciting students' ideas about creating simple electrical circuits. It then provides students with firsthand experiences to explore and collect data on how wires, batteries, and bulbs need to be organized in a simple circuit to transfer energy and make a bulb light.

MATERIALS NEEDED FOR THIS LESSON

- "Batteries, Bulbs, and Wires" formative assessment probe (included)

- Pieces of wire or aluminum foil

- Nonrechargeable AA battery

- Small replacement bulb for a flashlight that uses AA batteries (non-LED)

- PhET Circuit Construction Kit: DC simulation at http://phet.colorado.edu/sims/html/circuit-construction-kit-dc/latest/circuit-construction-kit-dc_en.html.

- Reading: *How Things Work: Lightbulbs* by Joanne Mattern (2016)

SAFETY NOTES

1. Have direct adult supervision while you are working on this activity.

2. Wear safety glasses with side shields or safety goggles during the setup, hands-on, and takedown segments of the activity.

3. Quickly pick up any materials used in this activity off the floor so they do not become a slip-and-fall or trip-and-fall hazard.

4. Use caution when using sharps (e.g., wires), which can cut or puncture skin.

5. Use caution when working with glass bulbs, which can shatter if dropped and cut or puncture skin.

6. Do not keep circuits connected to batteries for more than a minute. This has the potential to overheat the wiring and burn hands.

7. Wash your hands with soap and water after completing this activity.

Batteries, Bulbs, and Wires

  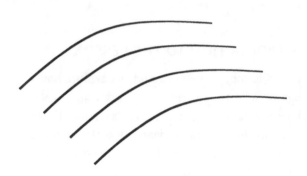

Kirsten has a battery and a small bulb. She wonders how many strips of wire she will need to connect the battery and the bulb so that the bulb will light. What is the *smallest number* of wire strips Kirsten needs to make the bulb light up?

A One strip of wire

B Two strips of wire

C Three strips of wire

D Four strips of wire

Explain your thinking about how to light the bulb. Draw a picture to support your explanation.

Picture:

"BATTERIES, BULBS AND WIRES" PROBE BACKGROUND INFORMATION

Teacher Explanation

The best answer is A: One strip of wire. If you closely examine a flashlight bulb, you will see two small wires sticking up in the bulb, connected by a very fine wire called a filament. The two wires on either side of the filament extend downward into the bulb's base, where you cannot see them through the metal casing that surrounds the bulb's base. One of these wires goes down to the very bottom of the base (the pointed end). The other wire is connected to the side of the metal base (which sometimes is ridged to screw into a socket). It is necessary to know where these wires end on the bulb's base—at the tip and the side—in order to use one wire to make a circuit that lights a bulb.

The battery, wire, and bulb need to be connected in such a way that they form a complete circuit. To do this, hold one end of the wire against the negative terminal of the battery (the bottom, or flat end). The other end of the wire should touch or wrap around the side of the metal casing that forms the base of the light bulb. With one end of the wire wrapped around the metal side of the bulb and the other end touching the bottom of the battery, touch the tip of the light bulb base to the positive terminal of the battery (bumpy end) and the bulb will light. The bulb lights with just one wire because the electricity flows out of the battery's negative terminal (flat bottom), through the wire to where it is attached to the side of the bulb's metal casing, up through one of the wires inside the bulb, across the filament, and down the other wire inside the bulb to where it is attached to the point on the base of the bulb that touches the positive terminal (the bump) of the battery, completing a full circuit.

Be aware, however, that students can choose the best answer, "One strip of wire," and still have an incorrect configuration of a circuit. For example, some students may touch one end of the wire to the battery and the other to the bulb, thinking the energy from the battery will flow through the wire to the bulb. Students who choose two wires as their answer may understand that a complete circuit is needed but not understand the internal configuration of a light bulb.

Research on Students' Ideas Related to This Probe

- Studies by Shipstone (1985), Arnold and Millar (1987), and Borges and Gilbert (1999) show that before instruction, many K–8 students are not aware of the bipolarity of batteries and light bulbs. As a result, they do not recognize the need for a complete circuit and have difficulty making a bulb light when provided with a battery and wires. Even high school and university students have difficulty with this task (AAAS 2007, pp. 26–27).

- Many students will use a source-consumer model, where the battery gives something to the bulb. In this context, younger students will often draw a single wire going from the top of the battery (unipolar model) to the bulb. Another model often used by both younger and older students involves two wires, each one going out of an end of the battery (bipolar model) and touching the bulb, with the electricity going from the battery to the bulb through each wire (Driver et al. 1994).

- Some students will regard one wire as the "active" wire and the second wire as a "safety wire" (Driver et al. 1994).

THREE-DIMENSIONAL LEARNING TARGETS FROM A *FRAMEWORK FOR K–12 SCIENCE EDUCATION*

Disciplinary Core Ideas: Grades 3–5: Energy can be transferred from place to place by sound, light, heat, and electrical currents. The energy transferred in a circuit can produce sound, heat, or light. *Grades 3–5*: Conservation of Energy and Energy Transfer: Energy can also be transferred from place to place by electric currents, which can then be used locally to produce motion, sound, heat, or light. The currents may have been produced by transforming the energy of motion into electrical energy.

Scientific Practices: Analyzing and Interpreting, Carrying Out Investigations, Constructing Explanations

Crosscutting Concepts: Patterns, Energy and Matter: Flow, Cycles, and Conservation

CONNECTIONS BETWEEN THE *FRAMEWORK*, FORMATIVE ASSESSMENT PROBE, AND *EXPLORE-BEFORE-EXPLAIN* LESSON

Before students connect energy transfer to how circuits work, they first **explore** how to make a simple circuit and **explain** how a battery, bulb, and wires need to be configured to make a bulb light. The "Batteries, Bulbs, and Wires" formative assessment probe elicits students' initial ideas about creating circuits, activates their interest in exploring how circuits are configured, and provides teachers with information about common misconceptions. As students collect data from their **exploration**, they look for patterns to help them revise their models and explain how circuits work. They circle back around to **explore** and look at how energy is transferred in a circuit. With teacher guidance, students can explain how a circuit works using the concept of energy flow.

VIGNETTE: EXPLORING "BATTERIES, BULBS, AND WIRES"

The unit on energy transformations and electricity starts with the "Batteries, Bulbs, and Wires" formative probe to elicit students' incoming ideas about making a bulb light (Keeley, Eberle, and Dorsey 2008, pp. 57–62). Once students had examined the probe and were clear about the questions, they were asked to draw their ideas. They were also told to draw additional scenarios different from their predictions and label whether they thought each would light the bulb. Students brainstormed the problem individually by writing or drawing their ideas on a sheet of paper. After 5 minutes, students got into groups of three and shared their ideas (see Figure 8.1).

Once everyone had made predictions, students received the materials to build a circuit, including a small light bulb from a flashlight, aluminum foil, and a nonrechargeable AA battery. (*Note*: We used pieces of aluminum foil instead of strips of wire.

Figure 8.1. *Student's Predictions About Lighting a Bulb Using Aluminum Foil, a Battery, and a Light Bulb*

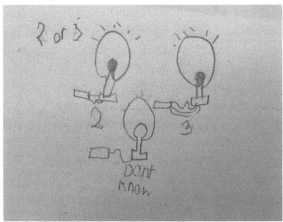

If you choose to do so, you will need to explain to students how to use the foil instead of wire.) The change in supplies from the original probe, with aluminum foil instead of wires, increased student interest by using common household materials from their daily lives in a face-to-face setting to test the probe with adult guidance. Students worked in pairs with the materials to perform the exploration and test various circuits. They were asked to test each scenario they had drawn regardless of whether they thought the bulb would light (see Figure 8.2).

Figure 8.2. *Student Trying to Make a Bulb Light Using a Piece of Aluminum Foil and a Battery*

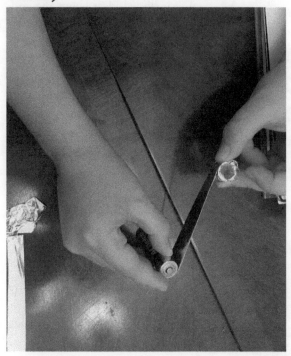

The bulb did not light, to students' surprise, when it was arranged in a straight-line circuit, with aluminum foil between the battery and the bulb. Once pairs of students tested their initial setup to see if the bulb did or did not light, they needed to

try other ways to light the bulb. Students were told to add notes to their drawings about their successful and unsuccessful attempts. As students collected evidence, they eventually figured out how to light the bulb. For example, they could light the bulb with two or three pieces of foil but needed their partners' help to form the complete circuit. In addition, they could use just one piece of aluminum foil to make the bulb light by creating a complete loop. Students were surprised by the results, as most of them had an inaccurate conception of a straight-line circuit. Very few students had predicted that to make a complete circuit, they needed to form a complete electrical loop, with aluminum foil from one terminal of the battery to the bulb and another piece of foil back from the bulb to the other battery terminal. Students noticed patterns in the data that served as evidence for the complete-loop configuration: They could make a bulb light using as little as one piece of aluminum foil as long as it made a complete loop.

When students understood the idea of a complete loop on a conceptual level, a microscopic investigation helped provide the underlying scientific principles. Students used the PhET Circuit Construction Kit: DC simulation at http://phet.colorado.edu/sims/html/circuit-construction-kit-dc/latest/circuit-construction-kit-dc_en.html. The simulation provided on-demand feedback, and students could see almost instantly whether they had made a complete electrical loop because the bulb would light up. When circuits did not form a complete loop, they would not light the blub (see Figure 8.3). More important, students learned content not easily observed firsthand. For example, they quickly noticed a key difference when creating a complete electrical loop compared with a straight lineup of battery-wire-bulb (see Figure 8.4). The critical difference was the movement of electrons (which they called electricity). Hence, students watch the energy stored in the battery move through the wires to the bulb and back to the battery when creating a complete electrical loop.

Explanation

The explanation started with a class reading of *How Things Work: Light Bulbs* (Mattern 2016). Students' firsthand experiences were reaffirmed early in the reading, which talked about electricity flowing through wires to light bulbs. Next, pages 8 and 9 stretched student understanding by explaining how an incandescent light bulb worked, requiring a complete loop versus a straight-line conception

Figure 8.3. *Student Using PhET Circuit Construction Kit: DC to Make a Circuit That Is Not a Complete Loop*

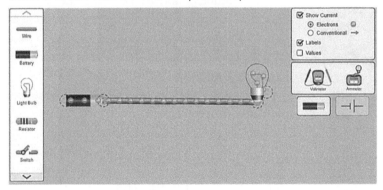

Figure 8.4. *Student Using PhET Circuit Construction Kit: DC to Make a Complete Electrical Loop and Light a Bulb*

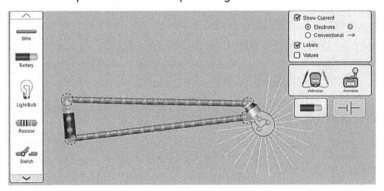

of an electrical circuit. Students then were asked to talk about how the inside of a light bulb was like their experiences making circuits. Blake explained to a partner that both have to "create an electrical loop." Finally, students also learned what it means when a light bulb goes out (the filament burned out) and about different types of bulbs.

Evaluation

Now that students could explain how wires, batteries, and bulbs must be configured to light the bulb, they revisited the probe, making new claims supported with evidence from their **explorations** to construct a **scientific explanation** that included ideas about the configuration of a bulb, battery, and wire. Students wrote that the bulb, aluminum foil, and battery must form a complete loop from the battery's negative terminal to the bulb and back to the battery's positive terminal to light the bulb. Students' claims were supported by evidence statements referencing their setups with battery, bulb, and aluminum foil that worked or did not work during their **explorations**. Finally, students were prompted to provide scientific reasoning that supported their new explanations of the probe using the crosscutting concepts of energy flow and cycles from their explorations using PhET.

Possible Further Elaborations

- Ask students to build models in PhET and then test them with wires, AA batteries, and bulbs. Consider challenging students to see if they can make two bulbs light and answer whether each bulb is brighter, less bright, or the same brightness as in their one-bulb systems.

- Have students build additional circuits: (1) When multiple bulbs are added, if one light goes out, all lights go out. (2) When multiple bulbs are added, if one light goes out, the other lights stay on. (These are not testable on PhET.) This elaboration activity aims to provide students with understanding about how electricity can flow and the impact of adding sources of electrical resistance in a circuit.

- An additional related probe that can be used to check for understanding is "How Can You Light the Bulb?" (Keeley and Harrington 2014).

REFERENCES

American Association for the Advancement of Science (AAAS). 2007. *Atlas of science literacy.* Vol. 2, Electricity and magnetism. Washington, DC: AAAS.

Arnold, M., and R. Millar. 1987. Being constructive: An alternative approach to the teaching of introductory ideas in electricity. *International Journal of Science Education* 9 (5): 553–563.

Borges, A., and J. Gilbert. 1999. Mental models of electricity. *International Journal of Science Education* 21 (1): 95–117.

Driver, R., A. Squires, P. Rushworth, and V. Wood-Robinson. 1994. Making sense of secondary science: Research into children's ideas. London: Routledge.

Keeley, P., F. Eberle, and C. Dorsey. 2008. *Uncovering student ideas in science, Volume 3: Another 25 formative assessment probes.* Arlington, VA: NSTA Press.

Keeley, P., and R. Harrington. 2014. *Uncovering student ideas in physical science, Volume 2: 39 new electricity and magnetism formative assessment probes.* Arlington, VA: NSTA Press.

Mattern, J. 2016. *How things work: Lightbulbs.* New York: Children's Press.

Shipstone, D. M. 1985. "Electricity in simple circuits." In *Children's Ideas in Science,* ed. R. Driver, E. Guesne, and A. Tiberghien, 33–51. Milton Keynes, UK: Open University Press.

9

EXPLORING
"What Is the Result of a Chemical Change?"

INTRODUCTION TO THE LESSON

In this lesson, elementary students **explore** what happens when vinegar and baking soda are mixed and **explain** that while the form of the products may appear different from the materials combined (reactants), the weight of the substances stays the same during a chemical reaction. The lesson is designed to provide students with firsthand experiences with data that serve as evidence to explain possible outcomes of a chemical reaction.

MATERIALS NEEDED FOR THIS LESSON

- "What Is the Result of a Chemical Change?" formative assessment probe (included)

- Baking soda

- Vinegar

- Balloon

- Small Erlenmeyer flask (50 ml) or clear glass bottle

- Electronic balance or digital kitchen scale

- Reading: *The Scoop About Measuring Matter* by Shirley Duke (2013)

- PhET Reactants, Products, and Leftovers at https://phet.colorado.edu/en/simulation/reactants-products-and-leftovers

- PhET Balancing Chemical Reactions at https://phet.colorado.edu/en/simulation/balancing-chemical-equations

SAFETY NOTES

1. Make sure you stand at a safe distance from the teacher's demonstration—about 15 feet or more.

2. The demonstrator is to wear indirectly vented chemical-splash safety goggles, nitrile gloves, and a nonlatex apron during the setup, hands-on, and takedown segments of the activity.

3. Observers are to wear indirectly vented chemical-splash safety goggles during the setup, hands-on, and takedown segments of the demonstration.

4. Quickly wipe up spilled or splashed vinegar off the floor so it does not become a slip-and-fall hazard.

5. Use caution with handling glass, which can shatter if dropped and cut or puncture skin.

6. Wash your hands with soap and water after completing this activity.

What Is the Result of a Chemical Change?

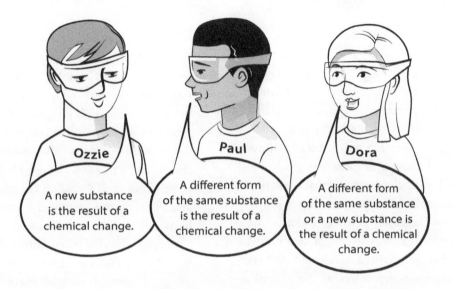

Ozzie: A new substance is the result of a chemical change.

Paul: A different form of the same substance is the result of a chemical change.

Dora: A different form of the same substance or a new substance is the result of a chemical change.

Which friend do you agree with the most? _____ Explain why you agree.

_____

_____

_____

_____

_____

_____

_____

_____

WHAT IS THE RESULT OF A CHEMICAL CHANGE?" PROBE BACKGROUND INFORMATION

Teacher Explanation

The best answer is Ozzie's: "A new substance is the result of a chemical change." During a chemical change, one or more substances react to form one or more new substances with different properties. The atoms from the original substances (reactants) are rearranged to form the new substances (products). There are many different types of chemical reactions, such as single substances that break down into two or more different substances, two or more substances that chemically combine to form a new substance, two substances in which one element replaces another element in a compound, and even different compounds that rearrange their atoms to form new compounds. In these examples, one or more new substances are formed that are chemically different from the original substances.

Research on Students' Ideas Related to This Probe

- Although in science the term chemical change refers to processes in which the reacting chemical substances transform into new substances, several studies have found that students often use the term to encompass a wide variety of changes, including physical transformations, especially when the color of a substance changes. How well students distinguish between chemical and physical changes may depend on their conception of the term substance. In general, students have difficulty understanding the idea of the chemical combination of elements until they can interpret what the combination means at a molecular level (Driver et al. 1994).

- Andersson (1991) investigated children's notions of chemical change and found they appear to fall into six categories: (1) it just happens; (2) matter just disappears; (3) the product materials must have been inside the starting materials; (4) the product material is just a modified form of the starting material; (5) the starting material just turns into the product material; and (6) the starting materials interact to form the product materials. Students experience difficulty discriminating consistently between a chemical change and a physical change. Evidence for this comes from several studies. For example, Ahtee and Varjola (1998) explored 13-to-20-year-olds' ideas about what kinds of things would indicate a chemical reaction had occurred. They found that about 20% of the 13-to-14-year-olds and 17-to-18-year-olds thought dissolving and change of state were chemical reactions. Only 14% of the 137 19-to-20-year-old university students in the study could explain what actually happened in a chemical reaction.

- Vogelezang (1987) found that students who regard ice as a different substance from water are likely to consider freezing water or melting ice as a chemical change. Briggs and Holding (1986) reported that 75% of the secondary students they sampled thought a change in mass was evidence for a chemical change. Stavridou and Solomonidou (1989) explored ideas held by Greek students ages 8 to 17 by presenting them with 18 different phenomena to classify as a chemical or physical change. They found that students who used the reversibility criterion were better able to distinguish between chemical and physical changes than students who did not consider reversibility. The students who used the reversibility criterion considered chemical changes to be irreversible, which could pose a problem in understanding chemical reactions.

Both groups used criteria that were macroscopic in character.

- Abraham, Williamson, and Westbrook (1994) found that students confused chemical and physical changes. There were indications that they had memorized the terminology rather than developed conceptual understanding.

- In a study by Abraham et al. (1992), eighth-grade students observed a chemical change in which a glass rod was held in the flame of a burning candle and a black film formed on the rod. To show understanding of chemical change, students were expected to identify that the transformation that took place and know that a new substance was formed, not just a different form of the same substance. Of the students questioned, some showed some understanding of chemical change, while others had some understanding of chemical change but then provided evidence of a physical change, and some of them said the change was not a chemical change because no chemicals were involved. And 70% showed no understanding that a chemical change had occurred with the burning of the candle and the formation of the black film on the glass rod.

THREE-DIMENSIONAL LEARNING TARGETS FROM *A FRAMEWORK FOR K–12 SCIENCE EDUCATION*

Disciplinary Core Ideas: Grades 3–5: When two or more different substances are mixed, a new substance with different properties may be formed. *Grades 3–5*: The amount (weight) of matter is conserved when it changes form, even in transitions in which it seems to vanish.

Science Practices: Carrying Out Investigations, Analyzing and Interpreting Data, Using Mathematical Thinking, Constructing Explanations

Crosscutting Concepts: Patterns, Cause and Effect

CONNECTIONS BETWEEN THE *FRAMEWORK*, FORMATIVE ASSESSMENT PROBE, AND *EXPLORE-BEFORE-EXPLAIN* LESSON

Before students connect that when substances react chemically, the weight of the substances stays the same, they first **explore** and **explain** how chemical reactions result in new substances with new properties. The "What Is the Result of a Chemical Change?" formative assessment probe elicits students' initial ideas about chemical reactions and motivates them to **explore** what happens to some materials when mixed. The probe provides teachers with information on students' commonly held ideas that will be challenged during the lesson. As students gather data from their **exploration**, they look for patterns and cause-and-effect relationships that help them explain what may happen during a chemical reaction. With teacher guidance, students can verify their understanding that weight stays the same after a chemical reaction. At the end of the lesson, students revisit the probe, revise their initial claims, and use a crosscutting concept to construct a scientific explanation with evidence from their investigation of the results of a chemical reaction.

VIGNETTE: EXPLORING "WHAT IS THE RESULT OF A CHEMICAL CHANGE?"

The lesson began by engaging students with the formative assessment probe "What Is the Result of a Chemical Change?" (Keeley and Cooper 2019, pp. 137–42). Students had a mix of ideas that reflected their understanding of the term substance. Most agreed with Paul or Dora, and some students claimed that "smoke will be produced during a chemical reaction." Students were asked whether the smoke would be the same as or different from the original materials. They thought that the smoke "would be a different form of the same material." Some suggested their explanation was similar to what occurs with water during a phase change. Aiden asserted that "regardless if water is ice, liquid, or gas, it's all water." In general, students had little experience thinking about chemical reactions, and most thought they would always produce "smoke," "fire," or an "explosion." Students also had not thought deeply about the materials that go into a chemical reaction (reactants) and the products.

To bridge the formative assessment probe with a testable experience, the class investigated a specific situation using everyday materials. The investigation centered around what students thought baking soda and vinegar would be like before and after being combined (see Figure 9.1).

Once students had made predictions about the probe, they passed around two beakers, one with 50 ml of vinegar and the other with 50 ml of baking soda. Students had various ideas of what the substances would look like and do when mixed. For example, many students thought the solution would "erupt" like a volcano (see Figures 9.2 and

Figure 9.1. *The Assessment Probe: Is It a Change?*

IS IT A CHANGE?

You are having an argument with your friend about what happens when you mix vinegar and baking soda.

Predict what will happen when you mix vinegar and baking soda below.

Before	After

1. **Which of the following best describes the results of the materials' masses? (Circle your prediction)**
   A. The mass of the materials will be more before the reaction takes place.
   B. The mass of the materials will be more after the reaction takes place.
   C. The mass of the materials will be the same before and after the reaction.

2. **Where did your ideas come from? (Circle all that apply)**

A. A book I read	G. My own experiences
B. A movie or television show	H. Other peoples' experiences
C. Talking with my friends or family experience	I. Things we did in class this year
D. Websites of videos	J. Things we did in other classes
E. Social media	K. Logic—it makes sense to me
F. Posters or other pictures	L. Evidence from observation

9.3). Other students thought that the baking soda would dissolve in the vinegar.

Students were asked follow-up content questions that dealt with changes in the weights of the materials. They had a range of ideas. About half thought that the weight would be higher before the reaction. No students thought the weight would be the same. The last question asked students to think about why they held certain conceptions (see

Figure 9.2. *One Student's Prediction About Is It a Change?*

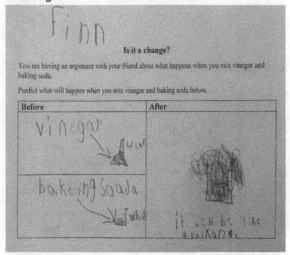

Figure 9.3. *Another Student's Prediction About Is It a Change?*

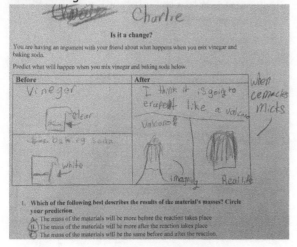

Keeley 2019). Most of the students' responses were related to their past lived experiences (items G, H, I, and J in Figure 9.1).

The preassessment data provide fascinating insights for teachers. For example, many students said they had seen this demonstration or something like it before in a different class. Interestingly, though students may have seen the demonstration before, their mixed conceptions indicate that their prior experiences did not promote long-lasting understanding. Thus, this was a ripe area for investigations to construct knowledge based on evidence students collected.

Once everyone had made a prediction, it was time to test their predictions. Doing this specific science investigation required that students wear indirectly vented chemical-splash goggles. Many students found that the initial demonstration confirmed their predictions and the solution bubbled (Figure 9.4). While the reaction was not as dramatic as they had hoped for (no eruption), the demonstration helped students focus on the cause-and-effect relationship evident in the chemical reaction.

Students considered the questions, "When baking soda and vinegar are mixed into a single solution, is a new and different substance created?" and "What evidence supports our ideas?" They were encouraged to talk about the before and after substances in terms of states of matter. Students explained that we mixed a solid (baking soda) to create a liquid and a gas. The bubbling and production of gas was an excellent way to target the crosscutting concept of cause and effect and provided some beginning evidence that the resulting substance had new and different properties, one being gas production. At this point, the class thought about whether gas has weight and how it could be measured. While the initial demonstration was anticlimactic, the conversation that followed intrigued students about the changes that would occur.

Figure 9.4. *Student's Observations About What Happens When Vinegar and Baking Soda Are Mixed*

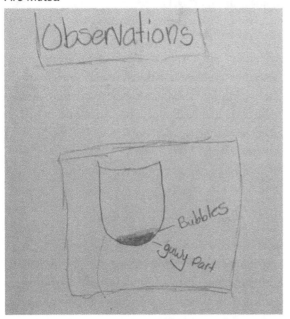

Figure 9.5. *Student's Observations and Data About Weight From the Flask-Balloon Setup*

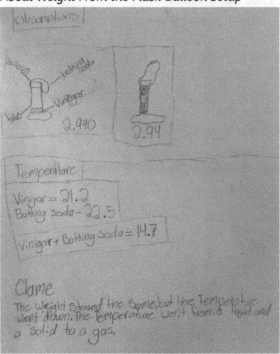

To investigate a weight change required a unique experimental setup. First, 50 ml of vinegar was placed in an Erlenmeyer flask (elementary teachers can use a clear glass bottle instead). Next, baking soda was placed in a balloon. The balloon was carefully stretched over the mouth of the Erlenmeyer flask, making sure not to mix the baking soda and vinegar. A small strip of black electrical tape was used to seal the balloon to the Erlenmeyer flask with no gaps. Finally, the flask-balloon setup was placed on an electronic balance. (See the teacher video resource at https://youtu.be/gIuJKE6eGpQ.) The chemical reaction was initiated when the balloon was lifted and the baking soda fell into the vinegar. The weight did not change, remaining at 2.94 g (see Figure 9.5). (*Note*: This demonstration is challenging to set up and mimics a closed system. Teachers should perform the demonstration beforehand, because the demonstration is performed on the electronic balance, and the system needs to be

as closed as possible. Also, as a cautionary note, teachers should wear protective goggles, a heavy-duty apron, and gloves.)

We also did the demonstration without sealing the container with a balloon to show students that gas has weight. Students measured the weight of the materials. When the substances were mixed, the weight was less than the total weight of the materials. Comparing the demonstrations provided students with evidence that gas has weight.

The data highlighted the importance of decimal places in measurement and was evidence needed to help formulate a claim. The focus on the crosscutting concept of scale, proportion, and quantity was a nice bridge to the CCSS mathematics standard that emphasizes students gaining abilities to represent "data set of measurements in fractions of a unit" (NGAC and CCSSO 2010; CCSS.Math.Content.5.MD.B.2).

Explanation

Students engaged in a read-aloud of a short excerpt from a 3–4 reader titled *The Scoop About Measuring Matter* (Duke 2013). This allowed them to build on their prior experiences and knowledge by providing accurate content from a reliable source. During the read-aloud, the teacher used the term "weight" in place of "mass" because this term is used as a stepping-stone to understanding mass in middle school.

> Mass [Weight] stays the same when an object changes physical properties, such as state, color, or shape. Mass [Weight] also stays the same in a chemical reaction when two combined materials change into entirely new materials.
>
> **The Law of Conservation of Mass [Weight]**
>
> In 1789, French chemist Antoine Lavoisier proved that mass [weight] put into a reaction equaled the mass [weight] that came out of the reaction. No new mass [weight]. No mass [weight] destroyed. Voila, you have the conservation of mass [weight] (Duke 2013, pp. 16–17).

Thus, students formed a more sophisticated understanding that the mass is conserved in a chemical reaction and learned that this property is termed the law of conservation of mass.

The short reading verified students' firsthand experiences with an explanation from a credible source. In addition, as a whole-class discussion, common indicators of chemical changes were listed, including the formation of gas bubbles, color change, and temperature change. Additional sources of evidence for chemical changes were identified, so students did not think gas was always produced in a chemical change. The goal was to wed students' firsthand experiences with data and teacher-led explanations, so student construction of knowledge would include more scientific understanding.

Evaluation

Once students experienced thinking about the materials before and after a chemical reaction, they revisited the "What Is the Result of a Chemical Change?" formative assessment probe and were asked to extend their explanation by explaining what happens to the weight of the substances formed during a chemical reaction. Many students agreed that a new substance results from a chemical change (Ozzie's idea). For example, Charlie explained, "I agree with Ozzie because when my teacher mixed baking soda and vinegar, it turned into a gas when baking soda is a solid and vinegar is a liquid." However, Kennedy added, "When we measured the materials, they were the same before and after."

Possible Further Elaborations

- Ask students to consider the "Will It Form a New Substance?" formative assessment probe (Keeley and Cooper 2019). Make sure students know that a new substance means the change results in new matter with a chemical makeup and properties that are different from those of the original matter. For younger students, eliminate answer choices they may not be familiar with. This probe can be used with the card sort strategy (Keeley 2016). Print each of the answer choices on a card. Have students work in small groups to sort the cards into two columns: changes in which new substances are formed and changes in which new substances are not formed. Ask questions such as the following: "What properties of this changed material are different from the original material? What properties are the same? Can you get the same material back again?"

REFERENCES

Abraham, M., E. Grzybowski, J. Renner, and E. Marek. 1992. Understandings and misunderstandings of eighth-graders of five chemistry concepts found in textbooks. *Journal of Research in Science Teaching* 29 (2): 105–120.

Abraham, M., V. Williamson, and S. Westbrook. 1994. A cross-age study of the understanding of five chemistry concepts. *Journal of Research in Science Teaching* 31 (2): 147–165.

Ahtee, M., and I. Varjola. 1998. Students' understanding of chemical reactions. *International Journal of Science Education* 20 (3): 305–316.

Andersson, B. 1991. Pupils' conception of matter and its transformations (age 12–16). *Studies in Science Education* 18 (1): 53–85.

Briggs, H., and B. Holding. 1986. *Aspects of secondary students' understanding of elementary ideas in chemistry.* Leeds, UK: Children's Learning in Science Project, University of Leeds.

Driver, R., A. Squires, P. Rushworth, and V. Wood-Robinson. 1994. *Making sense of secondary science: Research into children's ideas.* New York: Routledge.

Duke, S., ed. 2013. *The scoop about measuring matter.* Vero Beach, FL: Rourke Educational Media.

Keeley, P. 2016. *Science formative assessment, Volume 1: 75 practical strategies for linking assessment, instruction, and learning.* 2nd ed. Thousand Oaks, CA: Corwin Press.

Keeley, P., and S. Cooper. 2019. *Uncovering student ideas in physical science, Volume 3: 32 new matter and energy formative assessment probes.* Arlington, VA: NSTA Press.

National Governors Association Center for Best Practices and Council of Chief State School Officers (NGAC and CCSSO). 2010. *Common core state standards.* Washington, DC: NGAC and CCSSO.

Stavridou, H., and C. Solomonidou. 1989. Physical phenomena–chemical phenomena: Do pupils make the distinction? *International Journal of Science Education* 11 (1): 83–92.

Vogelezang, M. 1987. Development of the concept of "chemical substance": Some thoughts and arguments. *International Journal of Science Education* 9 (5): 519–528.

10

EXPLORING
"Can It Reflect Light?"

INTRODUCTION TO THE LESSON

In this lesson, elementary students **explore** how different objects reflect light and **explain** how light is reflected in different ways, depending on the property of the object. The lesson begins by engaging students' initial ideas about objects that reflect light. It then provides students with a firsthand opportunity to explore and collect data on how objects reflect light differently, depending on their properties, and learn about the role of light in how we see objects.

MATERIALS NEEDED FOR THIS LESSON

- "Can It Reflect Light?" formative assessment probe (included)
- Shiny, smooth objects, such as a handheld mirror, smooth square of aluminum foil, metal serving spoon, brand-new coin, square of satin or other fabric with a sheen, polished apple, piece of glossy paper
- Dull, nonsmooth objects, such as a gray stone, piece of cardboard, rusty metal, wood, russet potato, bark from a tree, crumpled nonglossy paper
- Flashlight, such as a Maglite, penlight with a concentrated beam, or smartphone with a flashlight app. (To use a standard wide flashlight, cover the glass with opaque paper with a small hole cut in the center to concentrate the beam.)

- Whiteboards or a shiny, smooth light-colored wall, or sheets of glossy reflective white paper taped to a wall
- A completely dark room or dark box with viewing hole cut in one side. (To use the latter, place an object in the box, and drape an opaque cloth or blanket over the viewer and box so that no light can enter.) Alternatively, cut a small hole in one end of a poster tube for students to look through.

SAFETY NOTES

1. Have direct adult supervision while you are working on this activity.

2. Use caution when moving in the area if lights are dimmed for this activity. Make sure all fragile items have been removed from the activity zone.

3. Wear safety glasses with side shields or safety goggles during the setup, hands-on, and takedown segments of the activity.

4. Use caution when handling sharps (e.g., metal or wood) to avoid cutting or puncturing skin.

5. Do not taste or eat any food used in this activity.

6. Wash your hands with soap and water after completing this activity.

Can It Reflect Light?

What types of objects or materials can reflect light? Put an X next to the things you think can reflect light.

___ water

___ gray rock

___ leaf

___ mirror   ___ dull metal

___ glass   ___ red apple

___ sand   ___ rough cardboard

___ potato skin   ___ the Moon   ___ milk

___ wax paper   ___ rusty nail   ___ bark on a tree

___ tomato soup   ___ clouds   ___ brand new penny

___ crumpled paper   ___ soil   ___ old tarnished penny

___ shiny metal   ___ wood   ___ smooth sheet of aluminum foil

Explain your thinking. Describe the "rule" or the reasoning you used to decide if something can reflect light.

_____

_____

_____

_____

_____

_____

_____

_____

"CAN IT REFLECT LIGHT?" PROBE BACKGROUND INFORMATION

Teacher Explanation

The best answer is that all objects and materials on the list can reflect light. We know they reflect light because we can see these objects and materials. An object or material can be seen when light is reflected from the object or material and enters our eyes. If an object or material did not reflect light, we would not be able to see it. Most materials absorb some wavelengths of light and reflect the rest. This explains why we see different colors. When we see white, all colors have been reflected. Materials reflect light differently. For example, a shiny, smooth object reflects light at a definite angle, while a rough object reflects light more diffusely and scatters the rays. This scattering makes some objects appear dull.

Research on Students' Ideas Related to This Probe

- Students' ideas about light reflection may be limited by the context in which they learned about the reflection of light or experienced reflection of light in their everyday lives. For example, if their experiences have been primarily with mirrors, students can think that only smooth or shiny things like a mirror can reflect light (Driver et al. 1994).

- Anderson and Smith (1983) revealed that students could describe light as bouncing off mirrors but not off other objects. A few students even lacked a conception of light bouncing or reflecting off any objects. The researchers also found that 61% of the children they questioned thought color to be a property of an object without realizing that it results from light being reflected from the object.

- A variety of alternative conceptual models are used by students to explain how we see an object. These models include (1) rays that go from an object to the eye, (2) the fact that light just helps us see better with no mention of how, (3) something goes from the eye to an object (the eye as the activator of vision), (4) something goes back and forth between the eye and an object, (5) light goes from a source to the eye (and may include reflection) to help us see, (6) an image enters the eye, (7) a contrast with dark helps us see, and (8) sight goes farther out when there is light (Driver et al. 1994).

THREE-DIMENSIONAL LEARNING TARGETS FROM A *FRAMEWORK FOR K–12 SCIENCE EDUCATION*

Disciplinary Core Idea: *Grades 3–5*: An object can be seen when light reflected from its surface enters the eye.

Scientific Practices: Developing and Using a Model, Planning and Carrying Out Investigations, Constructing Scientific Explanations

Crosscutting Concepts: Patterns, Cause and Effect

CONNECTIONS BETWEEN THE *FRAMEWORK*, FORMATIVE ASSESSMENT PROBE, AND *EXPLORE-BEFORE-EXPLAIN* LESSON

Before students connect the reflection of light to how we see objects, they first **explore** and **explain** how objects reflect light differently depending on their properties. The "Can It Reflect Light?" formative assessment probe elicits students' initial ideas about reflection, activates their interest in **exploring** how objects reflect light, and provides information to the teacher on students' commonly held ideas that mirror the research findings and will be challenged during the lesson. As students gather data from their **exploration**, they look for patterns that help them construct a revised or refined **explanation** of how objects reflect light. Then they cycle back to **explore** how they would see the objects without light, developing the generalization that we need light to see an object. Finally, with teacher guidance, students draw light ray models to show how light reflects off an object and enters our eyes, allowing us to see the object. At the end of the lesson, students revisit the probe, revise their initial claims, and use a crosscutting concept to construct a scientific explanation using evidence from their investigation and their conceptual understanding of the role of light in how we see objects.

VIGNETTE: EXPLORING "CAN IT REFLECT LIGHT?"

The lesson started with the "Can It Reflect Light" formative assessment probe (Keeley, Eberle, and Farrin 2005). Students had very similar ideas, as exemplified by this rule written by Charlie: "If it is shiny or a liquid, I think it can reflect light because it has a flat, smooth surface for light to shine off of. And liquids also are able to have light bounce off them." We set out to test students' rules using common materials from the probe. The room was darkened, and a piece of white poster board was used as a backdrop for the exploration. The teacher shone a flashlight near the white poster board but not directly at it. Then a mirror was placed in the beam of light from the flashlight. Students immediately saw a bright beam of light appear on the poster board. The teacher moved the mirror back and forth in front of the flashlight so students could see the bright beam moving back and forth on the white poster board. Next, the class explored whether a brown paper bag would have a similar

influence as the mirror. At first students wanted to claim that the paper bag did not reflect light. However, on closer inspection, they realized that it, too, created lighted portions on the white poster board, although the light was more scattered. Finley noted that when the paper bag was placed in front of the beam of light, it "made the shadows disappear on the board."

Additional tests were conducted to see how materials reflect light differently. A block of wood had similar results as the paper bag, and students again noticed that the darkness and shadow areas disappeared and the object became lighted. The last test involved foil. Like the mirror, the foil created a more brightly focused spot of white light on the poster board. However, students noticed that the spot was not "as bright" as from the mirror and "more spread out." Thus, the demonstration illustrated that various materials reflect light differently. The whole class discussed the similarities and differences between the explorations. The light on the whiteboard came from the interaction between the material placed in front of the flashlight and the beam of light. The whiteboard became lighted not because the flashlight was pointed at it, but because the light was reflected off the material onto the whiteboard. The term *reflection* was used to describe what students noticed during their explorations.

Students conducted another exploration to investigate whether they could see objects when no light was present. The goal was to get students to think about whether light reflection has anything to do with seeing objects. First, the class considered whether they could see anything in total darkness. All students believed they could see in total darkness, citing their experiences in a dark room in their house or outside at night. Students thought of bedrooms with the lights off and being outside at night as being in total darkness.

The teacher used a 3-meter poster tube holder as a demonstration for students to explore the investigative questions about seeing in the dark. First, the teacher made a small hole in one end cap of the poster tube holder. On the other end cap were taped small pieces of foil, paper bag, and waxed paper, as well as a penny. The materials taped to the end cap were placed on the floor, while the small opening in the end cap was toward the ceiling. One by one, students were asked to look through the tiny hole in the poster tube. Finally, students were asked to describe what they saw. They responded that they saw "darkness" and that "nothing" was in the tube. Next, the teacher removed the end cap with the small hole and shone a flashlight into the tube. Again, students looked through the tube; however, this time they could see the foil, paper bag, waxed paper, and penny. A similar exploration was done for additional objects, including an apple, rock, cup of water, and sand. Students could not see the objects in complete darkness for each test, but they could when the cap was removed and the teacher shone the light into the poster tube.

Explanation

With two data-producing experiences in mind, students were challenged to create a model of the rays of light that explained how they could see objects in the poster tube with light but not in darkness. First, students drew one of two main pictures. A few students drew a ray of light coming directly from the object to the eye (straight-line view). Others drew a light ray from the flashlight that bounced off the object and then came to the eye. Students with a straight-line view were probed to consider whether the material produced light. This guiding question led these students to consider their models and create a more scientifically accurate explanation that light must originate from a source (flashlight). Thus, students used the crosscutting concept of

cause and effect to explain the phenomenon—no light, no sight!

Evaluation

Now that students could explain how light is reflected off objects in different ways, allowing us to see things as shiny or dull, and have a model to explain the role of light in how we see objects, they revisited the "Can It Reflect Light?" formative assessment probe. This time, students checked all the materials, claiming that there "has to be light to see" and that "light bounces off an object to our eye so we can see it." Students were encouraged to draw one of the objects from the list and create a model supporting their new explanation. An additional probe that can be used for evaluation or to formatively check for conceptual understanding is "Apple in the Dark" (Keeley 2018).

Possible Further Elaborations

- Ask students to draw how a person sees a plain, shiny white piece of paper on a desk in front of them when light is hanging directly over the paper. Then ask them to draw how the paper reflects the light. Check to ensure that students' drawings do not show the light reflected in only one direction, toward the eye. Students should also know that light travels from the paper in more than one direction.

- Have students compare light reflecting off both smooth and crumpled aluminum foil onto a wall or piece of paper. Connect this with the analogy (a conceptual model) of a ball (representing light) bouncing on a smooth floor or pavement versus a bumpy surface. Take students outside to bounce a ball on smooth pavement and then compare how the ball bounces on gravel or other rough, bumpy surfaces. Connect the idea to what happens to light—bouncing at a definite angle versus bouncing in scattered directions.

• Have students observe what happens to their pupils when they are in a darkened room. Connect the widening of their pupils to the eyes trying to let in more light so they can see. Have students use this idea to explain how animals with wide pupils that hunt in the dark, such as owls and lemurs, can see their prey.

REFERENCES

Anderson, C., and E. Smith. 1983. *Children's conceptions of light and color: Developing the concepts of light and color.* Paper presented at the annual meeting of the American Educational Research Association, Montreal.

Driver, R., A. Squires, P. Rushworth, and V. Wood-Robinson, 1994. *Making sense of secondary science: Research into children's ideas.* London: Routledge.

Keeley, P. 2013. *Uncovering student ideas in primary science: 25 new formative assessment probes for grades K–2.* Arlington, VA: NTSA Press.

Keeley P. 2018. *Uncovering student ideas in science: 25 formative assessment probes.* 2nd edition. Arlington, VA: NSTA Press.

Keeley, P., F. Eberle, and L. Farrin. 2005. *Uncovering student ideas in science: 25 formative assessment probes.* Arlington, VA: NTSA Press.

11

EXPLORING THE
"Grand Canyon"

INTRODUCTION TO THE LESSON

In this lesson, elementary students **explore** how flowing water can move materials to **explain** the role of rivers in the process of weathering and erosion and the formation of the Grand Canyon. The lesson begins by engaging students' ideas about how the Grand Canyon might have formed. It then provides students with firsthand experiences to explore and collect data on how water might move different types and sizes of rocks and soil.

MATERIALS NEEDED FOR THIS LESSON

- "Grand Canyon" formative assessment probe (included)

- 2-liter bottles (five per group)

- Different earth materials: sand, sandy soil, red clay, pebbles, and loam

- Hand spray bottle

- Small and large beakers of water that can hold between 500 and 1000 ml of water

- Small piece of wood (approximately 1 meter long)

SAFETY NOTES

1. Have direct adult supervision while you are working on this activity.

2. Wear safety goggles and nonlatex aprons during the setup, hands-on, and takedown segments of the activity.

3. Quickly wipe up spilled or splashed water, or other material such as sand or dirt, off the floor so it does not become a slip-and-fall or trip-and-fall hazard.

4. Use caution while working with glass containers, which can shatter if dropped and cut or puncture skin.

5. Carry out this activity away from electrical receptacles, which can shock an individual if near water.

6. Wash your hands with soap and water after completing this activity.

Grand Canyon

Six friends were standing along the rim of the Grand Canyon. Looking down, they could see layers of rock and the Colorado River at the bottom. They wondered how the Grand Canyon formed. They each had a different idea. This is what they said:

Natara: I think the Grand Canyon was formed when Earth formed. It has just gotten bigger over time.

Cecil: I think the Grand Canyon formed from earthquakes that cracked open the land and pulled it apart.

Garth: I think the Colorado River and streams slowly carved out the Grand Canyon.

Robert: I think a huge flood rushed through the land and formed the Grand Canyon.

Kumiyo: I think the river got so heavy that it sunk down through the rock and formed the walls of the Grand Canyon.

Luna: I don't agree with any of your ideas. I think the Grand Canyon was formed in some other way.

Who do you think has the best idea? _____ Explain your thinking.

_____

_____

_____

"GRAND CANYON" PROBE BACKGROUND INFORMATION

Teacher Explanation

The best answer is Garth's: "I think the Colorado River and streams slowly carved out the Grand Canyon." The oldest rocks in the Grand Canyon are over 1 billion years old. Although several factors contributed to the formation of the Grand Canyon over a long time, the primary processes responsible for the canyon we see today are weathering and erosion by river systems. About 6 million years ago, the Colorado River began to cut through the upper rock layers. (*Note*: Although 6 million years is still the most widely accepted time frame for the onset of the carving of the Grand Canyon, some scientists have proposed that it may have begun around 16 million years ago.) This cutting process happened slowly, inch by inch, as water, wind, and ice weathered away pieces of rock—from small grains to large boulders—which were carried away by the Colorado River. Smaller side streams and tributaries branched off the Colorado River and carved out other sections of the Grand Canyon. As the Colorado River moves rock and sediment downriver, it scours the riverbed and carves away at the banks, thereby widening and deepening the river.

Research on Students' Ideas Related to This Probe

- Students of all ages may believe that Earth is the same now as when it was formed and that any changes must have been sudden and comprehensive (Freyberg 1985).

- Some students view Earth as static and unchanging (Cheek 2010).

- When interviewed about how a canyon was formed, some college students used catastrophic events in their explanation. For example, they believed that a catastrophic event such as a flood, earthquake, or volcano formed a canyon or that a canyon started with a catastrophic event and formed through river erosion. Some students also provided a biblical explanation of a giant flood (Sexton 2012).

- Some students think rivers get heavy and sink into Earth, thus carving out the land and the river (Mackintosh 2005).

THREE-DIMENSIONAL LEARNING TARGETS FROM A FRAMEWORK FOR K-12 SCIENCE EDUCATION

Disciplinary Core Idea: Grades 3–5: Earth Materials and Systems: Rainfall helps to shape the land and affects the types of living things found in a region. Water, ice, wind, living organisms, and gravity break rocks, soils, and sediments into smaller particles and move them around.

Scientific Practices: Carrying Out Investigations, Analyzing and Interpreting Data, Constructing Explanations

Crosscutting Concepts: Cause and Effect, Scale, Proportion, and Quantity.

CONNECTIONS BETWEEN THE FRAMEWORK, FORMATIVE ASSESSMENT PROBE, AND EXPLORE-BEFORE-EXPLAIN LESSON

Before learning how the Grand Canyon was formed, students first **explore** and **explain** how water can wear away and move different earth materials. The "Grand Canyon" formative assessment probe elicits students' ideas and provides teachers with ideas that can be challenged and elaborated on during the lesson. As students gather data from their **explorations**, they construct an **explanation** about whether water moves earth materials and how canyons form. They then learn information during a class read-aloud that helps their understanding become more sophisticated and enables them to come up with a scientific explanation of how the Grand Canyon formed. Finally, students revisit the probe at the end of the lesson and revise their initial ideas with a scientific description from the *explore-before-explain* experiences.

VIGNETTE: EXPLORING THE "GRAND CANYON"

First, the class watched a brief introductory clip about the Grand Canyon so that all students could visualize its expansiveness regardless of prior experiences. (The video is available at NationalGeographic.com/travel/national-parks/grand-canyon-national-park. Stop the clip before the video describes the age of the Grand Canyon and how it was formed. Alternatively, teachers can show students photographs of the Grand Canyon, making sure they see the Colorado River at the bottom of the canyon.) Then, with an image of the Grand Canyon in mind, students shifted gears to wondering about the "Grand Canyon" formative assessment probe (Keeley and Tucker 2016, pp. 107–10).

The probe led to some exciting conversations, and students had a range of views. Many students agreed with Cecil and thought that an earthquake pulled the land apart, citing their experiences making canyonlike structures in sand and soil. Some students agreed with Kumiyo and

thought the river had sunk over time. However, no students believed that water was the main factor and that over time, the Colorado River carved out the canyon.

The exploration was dedicated to collecting data and evidence to help students answer the question raised by the probe. Students worked in groups of three, each of which received five 2-liter bottles with a portion cut out so the bottle resembled a boat (see Figure 11.1), as well as a hand spray bottle and small and large beakers of water. A small piece of wood was placed underneath the bottom end of the bottles to raise one end and lower the other. Then students filled each bottle with a different earth material: sand, sandy soil, red clay, pebbles, or loam. The earth materials were on a table in the center of the room so everyone could retrieve them.

Students performed the investigations on white paper on our tabletops. They wore sanitized, indirectly vented chemical-splash goggles and lab aprons. The exploration could efficiently be conducted outside. Students' first tests used the spray bottles to simulate rainfall and test whether rain

Figure 11.1. *Overall Setup for the Grand Canyon Erosion Investigation*

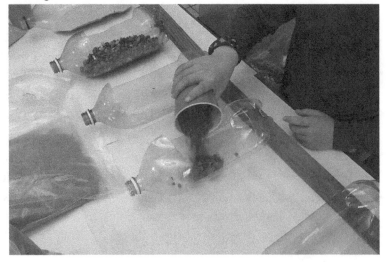

could break down the earth materials or move them to form a canyon.

Students quickly came to some scientific understandings. They were surprised when the water caused certain materials to break down while others remained intact. Almost immediately, a student said, "Look, I'm making a mini canyon" in the red clay soil. Another student remarked, "I'm making a canyon in the loam." They soon learned that how much earth material moved depended on the force and amount of water applied. Students saw that they could carve out a path in the sand, sandy soil, red clay, and loam but not the pebbles. They gained new insight on how much material water can move when they poured the water from the beakers more forcefully and in greater quantities. The loam was most easily displaced when water was forcefully added. At the end of the investigation, students were able to make evidence-based claims about how the water broke down and moved certain materials (red clay soil and loam), carved out a path in other materials (sand and sandy soil), and did nothing to others (pebbles).

Explanation

The data was qualitative, and the firsthand minds-on experiences allowed students to construct knowledge of Earth's process directly related to the overarching phenomenon—the formation of the Grand Canyon. The explanation began with a read-aloud of *Grand Canyon* (Chin 2017), during which students were prompted to connect their firsthand experiences with ideas from the reading. For example, just one page into the reading, students were introduced to the concepts of *erosion* and *weather*. In addition, students learned about phenomena that were connected to their firsthand experiences but not readily observable, such as that "rivers carve canyons" and that the process took "millions of

years … to form the mighty gorge known as the Grand Canyon" (Chin 2017).

Evaluation

Now that students could explain how water breaks rocks, soils, and sediments into smaller particles and move them around, they revisited the probe and made a new claim supported by evidence from their **explorations** and **explanations**. Students were able to pick the best response (i.e., Garth's) and use evidence from their explorations to develop scientific explanations about how water moved different types of earth materials. In addition, students used the crosscutting concept of scale, proportion, and quantity to explain that forming the Grand Canyon took millions of years based on what they learned from the reading.

Possible Further Elaborations

- Have students broaden their understanding of weather and erosion by investigating whether wind can move earth materials (sand, sandy soil, red clay, pebbles, loam). Students can blow through straws to simulate wind. Ask them to consider the similarities and differences between earth materials and whether they are more easily moved by water or wind.

- The formative assessment probe "Is It Erosion?" reveals whether students can distinguish between the processes of weathering and erosion (Keeley and Tucker 2016).

REFERENCES

Cheek, K. 2010. Commentary: A summary and analysis of twenty-seven years of geoscience conceptions research. *Journal of Geoscience Education* 58 (3): 122–134.

Chin, J. 2017. *Grand Canyon*. New York: Roaring Brook Press.

Freyberg, P. 1985. Implications across the curriculum. In *Learning in science: The implications of children's science*, ed. R. Osborne and P. Freyberg, 125–135. Auckland, NZ: Heinemann.

Keeley, P., and L. Tucker. 2016. *Uncovering student ideas in earth and environmental science: 32 new formative assessment probes*. Arlington, VA: NSTA Press.

Mackintosh, M. 2005. Children's understanding of rivers. *International Research in Geographical and Environmental Education* 14 (4): 316–322.

Sexton, J. 2012. College students' conception of the role of rivers in canyon formation. *Journal of Geoscience Education* 60 (2): 168–178.

Lessons Learned

Tackling your first *explore-before-explain* lesson may seem like an intimidating task, and we hope we have simplified the process. This book aims to help you make sense of using the *Uncovering Student Ideas* formative assessment probes in *explore-before-explain* teaching to develop lessons that promote students' conceptual understanding of the core ideas for elementary science described in *A Framework for K–12 Science Education* (NRC 2012). In addition, we hope we have sparked your thinking and reinvigorated your ideas about lesson planning.

While we as teachers want the learning experiences to be seamless from a student perspective, designing lessons can come from iteration (changing something that already exists) or invention (creating something original). Either iteration or invention is a great way to become an *explore-before-explain* teacher, and whichever we use, we can plan strategically and aim for new, better, and more cohesive student experiences. Once we understand the goals of *explore-before-explain* teaching, we can either iterate or invent to develop lessons for our students.

If we can begin our planning by thinking about experiences students could have that would allow them to construct accurate scientific knowledge, we can more easily situate learning. Said a bit differently, we can reflect on how to contextualize firsthand lessons around familiar phenomena. Once the firsthand experiences for students are grounded in a phenomenon, we can decide how to elicit their ideas and understandings and determine what explanations are necessary for them to gain deeper understandings of scientific principles. As the science storyline unfolds and students are learning during the lesson, elaborations help them understand more sophisticated ideas. The ultimate goal of using *explore-before-explain* teaching is to develop students' conceptual understanding to enable transfer learning. The following are key takeaways to help you on your journey to becoming an *explore-before-explain* teacher.

○— KEY TAKEAWAY 1 ⟶

START WITH WHAT YOU KNOW THROUGH EXPERIENCE AND ALREADY DO.

Thinking about your professional practices can initiate and simplify the process of becoming an *explore-before-explain* teacher by using what you know. Rather than starting from scratch based on the *Framework*, trying a new approach using something you already know is tried-and-true with students is often advantageous. Look for the successes in your instructional sequences and aim to scale them up. The most accessible and straightforward place to start from a lesson design standpoint may be by thinking of a firsthand activity that you currently use with students that helps them develop a conceptual understanding (iteration). Then consider whether you can shift the instructional script. There will be times when you can make a complete shift and have students conduct firsthand explorations before guiding them to explain the underlying scientific principles. Other times, you may need to modify your goals and focus on the conceptual understanding you hope students will construct. You can always go back and perform a more thorough investigation where students learn the nuanced details of the science under study.

You may be reluctant to flip the script because you think the exploration needs to be entirely student-driven without teacher guidance. This is not true. For example, you should explicitly teach procedures to help students think about doing science in valid and reliable ways (science and engineering practices). What you want to avoid in *explore-before-explain* instructional sequences is teaching concepts before students have first-hand experiences. You want students' content understanding to directly result from experiences doing science, using the SEPs and CCCs. Once you have pinpointed an evidence-based experience students can have in class, work backward to ask them about their prior knowledge and experiences related to the topic.

Finally, make sure students are aware of the specifics of what they are doing at all points in the learning process, and explain that science practices allow for the reliable interpretation of data. The result is that students will begin to build a complex conceptual understanding of the scientific phenomenon because they are organizing their content understanding based on direct encounters with evidence.

KEY TAKEAWAY 2

SELECT THE RIGHT WAY TO UNCOVER STUDENTS' IDEAS THAT MATCH THE EXPLORATIONS.

Selecting the right way to better uncover student ideas in an *explore-before-explain* instructional sequence is a curriculum-building process. You can work backward from a tried-and-true activity you have already used to find *Uncovering Student Ideas* probes that match the conceptual understanding you want your students to develop. Other times, starting with one of the probes is an easy way to promote students' learning, even though it may mean you have to do something new (invention). Many of these probes naturally translate into a straightforward investigation with firsthand experiences. You may find it beneficial to create a curriculum by using *Uncovering Student Ideas* probes to initiate the *explore-before-explain* lesson planning process.

The key point, whether you invent or iterate, is to carefully select ways to uncover student ideas that will allow students to transfer their thinking to data-based experiences, doing science to learn science. The *Uncovering Student Ideas* probes you select will ground student learning in the phenomenon. Moreover, irrespective of students' background knowledge and experiences, starting with an *Uncovering Student Ideas* probe allows students to explain and provide reasons for their ideas, creating an equitable playing field for all students. Regardless of the correctness of students' ideas, their firsthand experiences will allow them to develop a deeper conceptual understanding. All learning is a process. Some students will find their initial thoughts concerning the probes validated, while others will develop new or refined ideas based on the knowledge they construct firsthand through data-based experiences. Science often involves gradual revision, refinement, and at times even discarding of existing models or theories when new ones with greater explanatory power are presented—making learning about the process mirror the nature of science.

The probes should support a classroom culture of developing understanding instead of getting the right answer. Refrain from immediately correcting a student. Make it safe for students to share their ideas, whether they are right or wrong, knowing that everyone will eventually figure it out and discover the best way of thinking about a concept or phenomenon. If you refrain from giving answers early in the lesson, the *Uncovering Student Ideas* probes you select will be valuable as pre- and post-learning assessments for students, classes, and teachers. Probes should be used more than once, first as an initial elicitation and then after students have had the opportunity to build an understanding.

EMPHASIZE CLAIMS-EVIDENCE-REASONING.

If your goal is to develop students' conceptual understanding by using *Uncovering Student Ideas* probes aligned with the three dimensions of the *Framework*, then the assessment task must ask students to *apply* (i.e., transfer) their learning to new situations and *explain* the meanings they have made. Using the *Uncovering Student Ideas* formative assessment probes in *explore-before-explain* lesson planning means prioritizing experiences that allow students to construct claims-evidence-reasoning statements. It is not that how the *NGSS* aligns the three dimensions of the *Framework* is unimportant. Instead, you can better achieve the vision of the standards and modern learning theory by having a deliberate and focused goal to prioritize learning around students' evidence-based claims. Remember, a big idea behind how deeper conceptual understanding forms through *explore-before-explain* lessons is that "students who translate data → evidence → scientific claim perform difficult intellectual work like scientists. When students find patterns and causal relationships in the data, they have evidence for science sensemaking." The accumulation of data leads to evidence, which leads to scientific claims. Students must engage in logical and critical thinking at every link in the process—going from data to evidence and then from evidence to claim. When students notice patterns and relationships in data, they have evidence for science sensemaking. Thus, students' evidence-based claims illustrate what they know, understand, and can do. Because these evidence-based claims represent learning as evidenced by doing science, it is logical to use them to start setting up your instructional goals and to derive appropriate teaching and learning experiences.

In addition, the results you want to see for your students should directly tie to acceptable evidence of student learning. Students' evidence-based claims serve as an objective source of evidence of their proficiencies related to the three dimensions of the *Framework*. Starting with the evidence-based claims they can construct based on experiences may seem contrary to standard practice. Often, we consider standards first, then try to unpack them and what they might mean for learners, and only later develop a lesson or curriculum. One fallacy in interpreting the standards as the assessment goals is that teachers and curriculum developers often think they represent specific performance events that students should encounter during the unit of study. Instead, modern science standards represent the cumulative knowledge students gain during the grade span, and whether they are assessed is less critical than if they engage in science to learn by doing. Arguably, at some point in their future, if students learn by actively constructing science knowledge, they should transfer learning to illustrate understanding as described in modern standard documents. This view of conceptual understanding and transfer learning aligns with curriculum specialists' view of constructivist teaching and goal setting as priorities in lesson design (Wiggins and McTighe 2005).

BUILD EXPLANATIONS TO DEVELOP MORE SOPHISTICATED STUDENT UNDERSTANDING.

While students' evidence-based claims are essential for developing conceptual understanding, they are often insufficient to develop more scientifically literate students. Keep in mind that while explanations can be potent if new ideas fill gaps in understanding, students need a framework for incorporating new knowledge in valuable and comprehensible ways. Using the *Uncovering Student Ideas* formative assessment probes in *explore-before-explain* teaching, explanations are built on a conceptual understanding achieved by direct experiences with data that serve as evidence for understanding. Thinking about explanations might be different from what you are accustomed to. Many teachers are used to doing inform-type activities first to explain content. Remember, research shows that most teachers approach lesson planning with a standard script in which teacher explanation of content comes first, followed by verification and practice-type activities (Hofstein and Lunetta 2004).

The critical point is that explanations are time- and experience-sensitive and should answer *why* and *how* questions, especially ones students generate in their attempts to make meaning. Thus, a key factor in *explore-before-explain* teaching is guiding students to explain the underlying scientific principles. Challenge students to use simulations and text-based resources, engage in discussions that call on their conceptual knowledge, and use problem-solving and critical-thinking skills to explain scientific principles. When students work together, they can learn from the thinking representative of the class as a whole.

The goal for students is similar to expectations for 21st-century learners. With knowledge at our fingertips, there is value in finding resources that develop more sophisticated understanding. This means that students should play an active role in finding information that fills some gaps in understanding and evaluating the source's credibility. Explanations require a delicate balance. On the one hand, you can offer students some autonomy and guidance when exploring resources. On the other hand, you can provide direction to information not easily accessible from resources. There is too much information available to cover it all in

school—home in on ideas in the *Framework* and *NGSS* when planning explanations essential for students to develop deep conceptual understanding. Guiding students to explain their scientific reasoning helps them refine and elaborate their evidence-based claims. It is also a way to support their abilities in crucial SEPs, such as constructing explanations and communicating information, and serves as a building block to help them engage in argumentation from evidence.

If you wonder whether *explore-before-explain* is really so powerful for learners, think about why academic vocabulary and teacher, text, or simulation-based explanations are necessary. First, acquisition knowledge facilitates students' conceptual understanding and enables them to transfer ideas to new and different situations (McTighe and Silver 2020). Learning academic vocabulary, terms, and concepts about content and practices allows students to develop more sophisticated understanding and to gain science literacy by using science vocabulary. Second, some scientific principles are inherently abstract and thus inaccessible through firsthand explorations. For example, many particle-level ideas need an explanation to prepare students for more elaborated understandings. Finally, it would be inefficient and unnecessary to have students learn abstract scientific principles (which took scientists hundreds of years to formulate) solely through discovery-based approaches. Said a bit differently, students do not have to discover all the science content in your curriculum from firsthand experience alone. Teachers play an essential role in developing conceptual understanding by introducing explanations at the right time for learners.

○─ KEY TAKEAWAY 5 ──→

WHILE STANDARDS ARE ESSENTIAL, THEY ARE NOT CURRICULUM.

Becoming an *explore-before-explain* teacher requires thinking about teaching and learning in new ways. For many, the research and standards alone are not enough to develop an *explore-before-explain* mindset to teaching. Identifying the key learning goals, developing effective instructional strategies, and creating meaningful assessments are all critical parts of curriculum development. The *Framework* presents a modern vision for science education. Its three-dimensional construct calls for teachers to favor depth over breadth while engaging students in doing science, not just learning science facts. To avoid the familiar problem of curricula that are "a mile wide and an inch deep," the standards call for framing teaching around core ("big") ideas, science and engineering practices, and crosscutting concepts. Focusing on fewer, more significant ideas is critical to avoid superficial coverage while allowing more time to engage students in the kinds of active meaning-making processes necessary for developing conceptual understandings. Moreover, by streamlining the curriculum content, you will have more opportunities to involve students in learning and applying science practices.

Your job, whether as a teacher or part of a curriculum team, is to use the core ideas and science practices to design the specific pathway for teaching and learning. In *Understanding by Design* (2005), Wiggins and McTighe suggest using the desired teaching and planning activities to best achieve the intended learning outcomes. These first considerations are about deciding on instructional priorities, including targeting a unit's learning goals that identify what you want students to know, understand, and do. This means framing lessons around understandable phenomena through data-based experiences. Focus goals specifically on what students should do with their learning in the long run. Here is the place to prioritize the processes involved in doing science, thinking about data, and identifying the big ideas students should come to understand while completing the unit. This emphasis is entirely in sync with the recommendation of the *Framework* and *NGSS* to center science teaching around DCIs, SEPs, and CCCs.

CONCLUSIONS

We hope that the model lessons, research, and tips for designing research-based strategies motivate you to use the *Uncovering Student Ideas* probes in an *explore-before-explain* sequence for science teaching. Starting the journey of becoming an *explore-before-explain* teacher is a rewarding professional process that forces you to consider the best possible ways to ensure that students gain high levels of learning. Your students will benefit from a more robust and relevant understanding of science and the ability to organize their understandings based on direct experiences. We encourage you to create foundational situations in which students can construct knowledge of science phenomena with data and evidence-based firsthand experiences. We wish you the best of luck as you use *Uncovering Student Ideas* probes in your *explore-before-explain* teaching to take student learning to new levels in your classrooms and schools.

REFERENCES

Hofstein, A., and V. N. Lunetta. 2004. The laboratory in science education: Foundation for the 21st century. *Science Education* 88 (1): 28–54.

McTighe, J., and H. Silver. 2020. *Teaching for deeper learning: Tools to engage students in meaning making.* Alexandria, VA: ASCD.

National Research Council (NRC). 2012. *A framework for K–12 science education: Practices, crosscutting concepts, and core ideas.* Washington, DC: National Academies Press.

Wiggins, G., and J. McTighe. 2005. *Understanding by design.* Expanded 2nd ed. Alexandria, VA: ASCD.

Index